TABLE OF CON

The Quilter's Patch Color Wheel	2	Moon Flower Block	52
Exploring the Quilter's Toolbox	3	Sweet Pea Block	58
Applique & Embroidery Methods	4	Bachelor Button Block	62
Cosmos Block	6	Hollyhock Block	66
Delphiniums Block	8	Greenhouse Block	72
Cat Block	12	Sunflower Block	78
Nine Patch Daisy Block	16	Butterfly Blocks	82
Sidewalk and Log Cabin Roses Block	20	Fence Block	84
Petunias Block	24	Quilt Center & Borders	88
Tulips Block	28	Applique & Embroidery	100
Daylily Block	32	Binding & Backing	107
Dahlia Block	36	Templates	108
Honeysuckle Block	42	Silver Linings in Color	116
Coneflower Block	46	Block of the Month Detail	117

EXPLORING THE QUILTER'S TOOLBOX

Dear Quilting Friends,

Welcome to the Quilter's Patch! My vision for this book is to help you plan and grow a beautiful quilt garden. Just like in gardening, there are tools to help you become successful. Explore your tool box and get ready to garden!

Start planting your garden and watch it grow with every patch. With each step, you will grow, refresh your skills and become more precise. I hope you will challenge yourself by trying something you have not done before and enjoy learning new techniques. Give every block some TLC!

If there are some blocks you like more than others, you can plant your quilt garden exactly to your liking! Make multiples of your favorites or use all of the blocks; it is your own personal garden. You can create a few blocks and use them as framed pieces or pillows, or make them all to create your Quilter's Patch garden quilt.

When selecting fabrics for a project, I often rely on my rule of five. I make sure to select prints from five groups to ensure a well-balanced but interesting combination: large prints, medium prints, small prints, stripes and polka dots. But, when I'm working with a fabric palette of solids or small prints like the Silver Linings in Color collection that I use for the Quilter's Patch quilt, I use both a color wheel and nature to make the right selection.

With a color wheel, I choose colors directly across from one another to give the greatest contrast but also the greatest complement. Using complementary colors will help you pair colors and choose warm and cool colors that go well together. And when in my garden, I appreciate the beauty of the fine color variations in a flower's stem and use that inspiration to choose similar colors for my quilts. These tools will put you on the right path to a successful block or quilt.

Come quilt with me,

Edyta

Machine Applique

- Carefully trace all of the shapes for applique onto the matte side of freezer paper.

- Cut all of the freezer paper pieces on the traced line. Cut edges in a smooth manner. This ensures an even and lovely applique. Uneven cutting will make uneven edges on your fabric pieces.

- Use a touch of a glue stick on the matte side of the freezer paper pattern and attach it to the wrong side of your applique fabric.

- Cut the fabric carefully around the shape, leaving no more than ¼". Snip in ³⁄₁₆" on all edges ½" apart to allow the fabric to effortlessly fold in, being careful not to cut too close to the paper pattern. Use the tip of your iron on a cotton dry setting to turn under the ¼" allowance of your applique pieces. Hold the edge under for a few seconds to allow the fabric to adhere to the shiny side of the freezer paper. Continue until all edges are turned under. For a circle shape, use a basting stitch around the ¼" seam allowance of the applique piece, and pull the stitches together. Press.

- Once all of the applique pieces are ready, it is time to assemble the block. Prepare your background fabric by starching and pressing.

- With a touch of glue, attach your pieces to the quilt top.

- Use your iron to press and secure all applique pieces in place. The shiny side of the freezer paper will allow the applique pieces to stick to the quilt top.

- To machine applique, I use invisible thread (100% clear nylon) with a 0 tension on the top, beige cotton thread in the bobbin, a size #90 needle and a tiny zigzag stitch. As you zigzag, make sure that the needle grabs the applique and the background fabric alternately.

- Make sure your machine is not bringing up the bobbin thread to the top of your applique. Lower the top tension if necessary. Gently press the block from the back which will heal holes from your zigzag stitch. Be careful not to overheat.

- With very sharp scissors, make a small slit in the background fabric under the applique pieces and remove the freezer paper.

Hand Applique

- Prepare the pieces following the machine applique instructions.

- Once you are ready to secure the pieces to the background, use silk thread and an applique needle.

- Position pieces on the background following the block or quilt layout.

- With a small whip stitch, sew around the edges of all pieces.

Fusible Applique

All shapes will need to be reversed for this technique.

- Trace the pieces onto lightweight fusible webbing.

- Cut out the shapes leaving ⅛" fusible webbing around the outside of the shapes.

- Press each piece to the wrong side of your fabric following the webbing manufacturer's directions. Do not overheat fusible webbing!

- Cut the fabric shapes to the outline of the pattern.

- Peel the paper from the back of the fabric shapes and position the pieces in place.

- Once all of the pieces are in place, press them gently with your iron.

- To sew the pieces, use invisible thread (100% clear nylon) with a 0 tension on the top, beige cotton thread in the bobbin, a size #90 needle and a tiny zigzag stitch. As you zigzag, make sure that the needle grabs the applique and the background fabric alternately.

- Make sure your machine is not bringing up the bobbin thread to the top of your applique. Lower the top tension if necessary. Gently press the block from the back which will heal holes from your zigzag stitch. Again be careful not to overheat.

Stem Stitch

- Use three strands of embroidery floss.
- Follow the stitch diagram below.

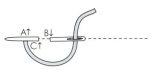

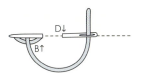

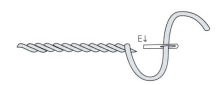

> **Throughout the book:**
> - **Use a ¼" seam allowance.**
> - **Press in the direction of the arrows.**

COSMOS BLOCK

Make 1. 12 ½" x 12 ½" unfinished.

42268-12   42264-39   42260-31   42261-38   42262-38   42265-27

Edyta's Tips:

Using fabrics in different shades of the same color adds dimension and texture to your blocks.

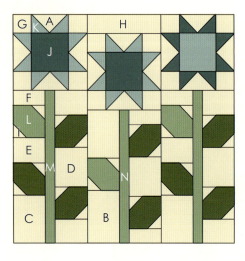

Fabric Requirements:

Background One Fat Quarter (18" x 21")	Fabrics A to I
Flowers Two 10" squares	Fabrics J & K
Leaves Two 10" squares	Fabric L
Stems One 10" square	Fabrics M & N

Cutting:

Background

1 - 3 ¼" x 21" strip, subcut into:
    3 - 3 ¼" squares (A) *Cut each on the diagonal twice*
    1 - 2 ¼" x 3 ¼" rectangle (B)
    3 - 2 ¼" x 3" rectangles (C)

2 - 2 ¼" x 21" strips, subcut into:
    3 - 2 ¼" x 2 ½" rectangles (D)
    6 - 1 ¾" x 2 ¼" rectangles (E)
    4 - 1 ¼" x 2 ¼" rectangles (F)

2 - 1 ½" x 21" strips, subcut into:
    12 - 1 ½" squares (G)
    1 - 1 ½" x 4 ½" rectangle (H)

2 - 1 ¼" x 21" strips, subcut into:
    22 - 1 ¼" squares (I)

Flowers - from one fabric cut
    1 - 2 ½" square (J)
    8 - 1 ⅞" squares (K) *Cut each on the diagonal once*

Flowers - from one fabric cut
    2 - 2 ½" squares (J)
    4 - 1 ⅞" squares (K) *Cut each on the diagonal once*

Leaves - from one fabric cut
    8 - 2 ¼" squares (L)

Leaves - from one fabric cut
    3 - 2 ¼" squares (L)

Stems
    2 - 1" x 8 ½" rectangles (M)
    1 - 1" x 7 ½" rectangle (N)

Construction:

1 Assemble two matching Fabric K triangles and one Fabric A triangle.

Make 12 Flying Geese Units.
1 ½" x 2 ½" unfinished.

2 Assemble four Fabric G squares, four matching Flying Geese Units and one Fabric J square.

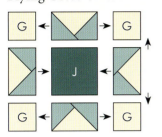 

Make 3 Star Units.
4 ½" x 4 ½" unfinished.

3 Draw a diagonal line on the wrong side of the Fabric I squares.

With right sides facing, layer a Fabric I square on the bottom left corner of a Fabric L square.

Stitch on the drawn line and trim ¼" away from the seam.

Repeat on the top right corner.

Make 11 Leaf Units.
2 ¼" x 2 ¼" unfinished.

4 Assemble one Fabric F rectangle, four Leaf Units, three Fabric E rectangles, one Fabric C rectangle, one Fabric M rectangle and one Fabric D rectangle.

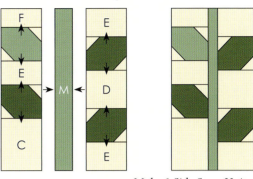

Make 2 Side Stem Units.
4 ½" x 8 ½" unfinished.

5 Assemble one Fabric C rectangle, three Leaf Units, the Fabric B rectangle, the Fabric N rectangle, two Fabric F rectangles and one Fabric D rectangle.

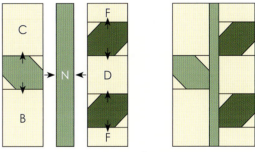

Make 1 Center Stem Unit.
4 ½" x 7 ½" unfinished.

6 Assemble three Star Units, two Side Stem Units, the Fabric H rectangle and the Center Stem Unit.

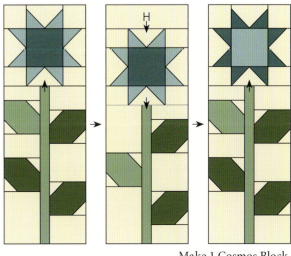

Make 1 Cosmos Block.
12 ½" x 12 ½" unfinished.

Make 1. 12 ½" x 12 ½" unfinished.

42260-12 42268-44 42261-36 42260-31 42261-38 42266-30

Fabric Requirements:

| Background | Fabrics A to O |
| One Fat Quarter (18" x 21") | |

| Flowers | Fabrics P to T |
| Three 10" squares | |

| Stems and Leaves | Fabrics U, V & W |
| Two 10" squares | |

Edyta's Tips:

Press your seam allowances in opposite directions so your seams will "nest" with each other and lie nice and flat.

Cutting:

Background

1 - 2 ⅝" x 21" strip, subcut into:
- 2 - 2 ⅝" squares (A)
- 2 - 2 ¼" x 2 ½" rectangles (B)
- 3 - 2 ¼" squares (C)

1 - 2 ⅛" x 21" strip, subcut into:
- 3 - 2 ⅛" squares (D)
- 1 - 2" x 2 ¼" rectangle (E)

1 - 1 ¾" x 21" strip, subcut into:
- 3 - 1 ¾" x 2 ¼" rectangles (F)
- 6 - 1 ¾" x 2" rectangles (G)

4 - 1 ½" x 21" strips, subcut into:
- 6 - 1 ½" x 4 ½" rectangles (H)
- 6 - 1 ½" x 2" rectangles (I)
- 12 - 1 ½" squares (J)
- 3 - 1 ¼" x 2 ¼" rectangles (K)
- 6 - 1 ¼" squares (L)

2 - 1" x 21" strips, subcut into:
- 1 - 1" x 12 ½" rectangle (M)
- 5 - 1" x 1 ¾" rectangles (N)
- 6 - 1" squares (O)

Flowers - from one fabric cut
- 6 - 1 ½" squares (P)

Flowers - from one fabric cut
- 6 - 1 ½" squares (Q)
- 3 - 1 ¼" squares (R)

Flowers - from one fabric cut
- 3 - 1 ¼" squares (S)
- 6 - 1" squares (T)

Stems and Leaves - from one fabric cut
- 2 - 2 ⅝" squares (U)
- 2 - 1" x 5 ½" rectangles (W)

Stems and Leaves - from one fabric cut
- 3 - 2 ⅛" squares (V)
- 1 - 1" x 5 ½" rectangle (W)

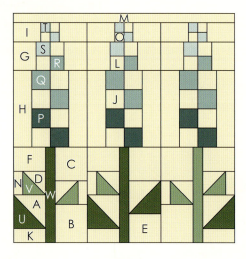

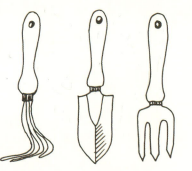

Construction:

1 Assemble two Fabric T squares and two Fabric O squares.

Make 3 Partial Small Flower Units.
1 ½" x 1 ½" unfinished.

2 Assemble two Fabric I rectangles and one Partial Small Flower Unit.

Make 3 Small Flower Units.
1 ½" x 4 ½" unfinished.

3 Assemble one Fabric S square, two Fabric L squares and one Fabric R square.

Make 3 Partial Medium Flower Units.
2" x 2" unfinished.

4 Assemble two Fabric G rectangles and one Partial Medium Flower Unit.

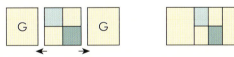

Make 3 Medium Flower Units.
2" x 4 ½" unfinished.

5 Assemble two Fabric Q squares, four Fabric J squares and two Fabric P squares.

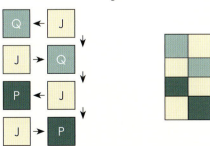

Make 3 Partial Large Flower Units.
2 ½" x 4 ½" unfinished.

6 Assemble two Fabric H rectangles and one Partial Large Flower Unit.

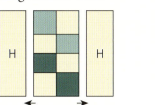

Make 3 Large Flower Units.
4 ½" x 4 ½" unfinished.

7 Draw a diagonal line on the wrong side of the Fabric D squares.

With right sides facing, layer a Fabric D square with a Fabric V square.

Stitch ¼" from each side of the drawn line.

Cut apart on the marked line.

One of the Small Leaf Units will not be used.

Make 6 Small Leaf Units.
1 ¾" x 1 ¾" unfinished.

8 Draw a diagonal line on the wrong side of the Fabric A squares.

With right sides facing, layer a Fabric A square with a Fabric U square.

Stitch ¼" from each side of the drawn line.

Cut apart on the marked line.

Make 4 Large Leaf Units.
2 ¼" x 2 ¼" unfinished.

9 Assemble one Fabric F rectangle, one Fabric N rectangle, one Small Leaf Unit, one Large Leaf Unit and one Fabric K rectangle.

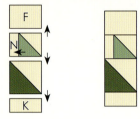

Make 2 Leaves One Units.
2 ¼" x 5 ½" unfinished.

10 Assemble one Fabric C square, one Small Leaf Unit, one Fabric N rectangle and one Fabric B rectangle.

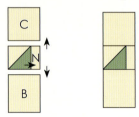

Make 1 Leaves Two Unit.
2 ¼" x 5 ½" unfinished.

11 Assemble one Fabric C square, one Large Leaf Unit and the Fabric E rectangle.

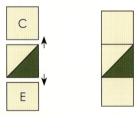

Make 1 Leaves Three Unit.
2 ¼" x 5 ½" unfinished.

12 Assemble one Fabric C square, one Fabric N rectangle, one Small Leaf Unit and one Fabric B rectangle.

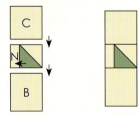

Make 1 Leaves Four Unit.
2 ¼" x 5 ½" unfinished.

13 Assemble one Fabric F rectangle, one Small Leaf Unit, one Fabric N rectangle, one Large Leaf Unit and one Fabric K rectangle.

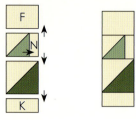

Make 1 Leaves Five Unit.
2 ¼" x 5 ½" unfinished.

14 Assemble one Leaves One Unit, one Fabric W rectangle and the Leaves Two Unit.

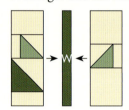

Make 1 Stem One Unit.
4 ½" x 5 ½" unfinished.

15 Assemble one Small Flower Unit, one Medium Flower Unit, one Large Flower Unit and the Stem One Unit.

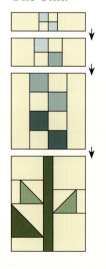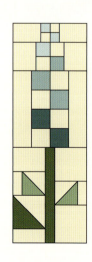

Make 1 Left Flower Unit.
4 ½" x 12" unfinished.

16 Assemble one Leaves One Unit, one Fabric W rectangle and the Leaves Three Unit.

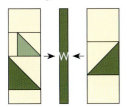 

Make 1 Stem Two Unit.
4 ½" x 5 ½" unfinished.

17 Assemble one Small Flower Unit, one Medium Flower Unit, one Large Flower Unit and the Stem Two Unit.

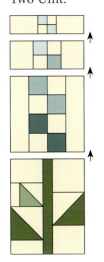 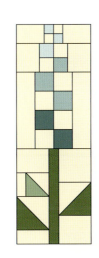

Make 1 Center Flower Unit.
4 ½" x 12" unfinished.

18 Assemble the Leaves Four Unit, one Fabric W rectangle and the Leaves Five Unit.

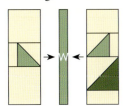 

Make 1 Stem Three Unit.
4 ½" x 5 ½" unfinished.

19 Assemble one Small Flower Unit, one Medium Flower Unit, one Large Flower Unit and the Stem Three Unit.

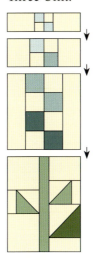 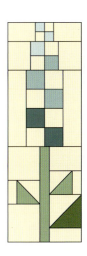

Make 1 Right Flower Unit.
4 ½" x 12" unfinished.

20 Assemble the Fabric M rectangle, the Left Flower Unit, the Center Flower Unit and the Right Flower Unit.

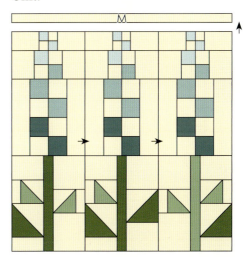

Make 1 Delphiniums Block.
12 ½" x 12 ½" unfinished.

CAT BLOCK

Make 1. 12 ½" x 12 ½" unfinished.

42266-12   42262-24   42266-20   42264-39

Fabric Requirements:

Background	Fabrics A to D
One Fat Eighth (9" x 21")	
Light Cat	Fabrics E, F & G
One 10" square	
Dark Cat	Fabrics H to L
One 10" x 15" rectangle	
Bow	Fabric M
One 10" square	

Edyta's Tips:

Before starting any project, always check your machine's ¼" seam allowance for perfect piecing.

Cutting:

Background

1 - 2 ⅞" x 21" strip, subcut into:
    4 - 2 ⅞" squares (A)

2 - 2 ½" x 21" strips, subcut into:
    1 - 2 ½" x 8 ½" rectangle (B)
    3 - 2 ½" x 4 ½" rectangles (C)
    4 - 2 ½" squares (D)

Light Cat

    3 - 2 ⅞" squares (E)
    2 - 2 ½" squares (F)
    2 - 1 ½" x 4 ½" rectangles (G)

Dark Cat

    1 - 2 ⅞" square (H)
    1 - 2 ½" x 8 ½" rectangle (I)
    1 - 2 ½" x 6 ½" rectangle (J)
    1 - 2 ½" x 4 ½" rectangle (K)
    2 - 1 ½" x 4 ½" rectangles (L)

Bow

    2 - 2 ½" squares (M)

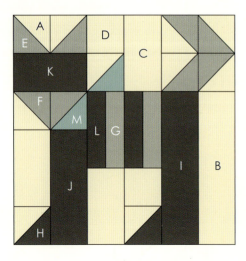

Construction:

1 Draw a diagonal line on the wrong side of the Fabric A squares.

With right sides facing, layer a Fabric A square with a Fabric E square.

Stitch ¼" from each side of the drawn line.

Cut apart on the marked line.

Make 6 Half Square Triangle One Units.
2 ½" x 2 ½" unfinished.

2 With right sides facing, layer a Fabric A square with the Fabric H square.

Stitch ¼" from each side of the drawn line.

Cut apart on the marked line.

Make 2 Half Square Triangle Two Units.
2 ½" x 2 ½" unfinished.

3 Draw a diagonal line on the wrong side of two Fabric D squares.

With right sides facing, layer a marked Fabric D square with a Fabric F square.

Stitch on the drawn line and trim ¼" away from the seam.

Make 1 Half Square Triangle Three Unit.
2 ½" x 2 ½" unfinished.

4 With right sides facing, layer a marked Fabric D square with a Fabric M square.

Stitch on the drawn line and trim ¼" away from the seam.

Make 1 Half Square Triangle Four Unit.
2 ½" x 2 ½" unfinished.

5 Draw a diagonal line on the wrong side of the remaining Fabric F square.

With right sides facing, layer the marked Fabric F square with the remaining Fabric M square.

Stitch on the drawn line and trim ¼" away from the seam.

Make 1 Half Square Triangle Five Unit.
2 ½" x 2 ½" unfinished.

6 Assemble two Half Square Triangle One Units and the Fabric K rectangle.

Make 1 Top Left Cat Unit.
4 ½" x 4 ½" unfinished.

7 Assemble the Top Left Cat Unit, one Fabric D square, the Half Square Triangle Four Unit, one Fabric C rectangle and four Half Square Triangle One Units.

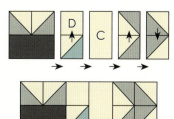

Make 1 Top Cat Unit.
4 ½" x 12 ½" unfinished.

8   Assemble one Fabric L rectangle and one Fabric G rectangle.

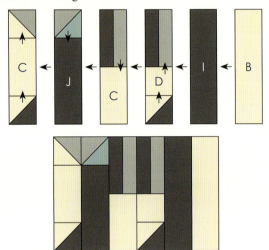

Make 2 Cat Stripe Units.
2 ½" x 4 ½" unfinished.

9   Assemble the Half Square Triangle Three Unit, two Fabric C rectangles, two Half Square Triangle Two Units, the Half Square Triangle Five Unit, the Fabric J rectangle, two Cat Stripe Units, one Fabric D square, the Fabric I rectangle and the Fabric B rectangle.

Make 1 Bottom Cat Unit.
8 ½" x 12 ½" unfinished.

10   Assemble the Top Cat Unit and the Bottom Cat Unit.

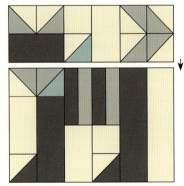

Make 1 Cat Block.
12 ½" x 12 ½" unfinished.

Make 1. 12 ½" x 12 ½" unfinished.

42267-12   42260-31   42261-37   42268-50   42261-38   42265-27

Fabric Requirements:

Background One Fat Quarter (18" x 21")	Fabrics A to P
Flowers Two 10" squares	Fabrics Q & R
Flower Accent One 10" square	Fabrics S & T
Stems and Leaves One 10" squarc	Fabrics U to Y
Leaves One 10" square	Fabrics U & V

Edyta's Tips:

Press your seam allowances to the darker fabrics to make sure they don't show through the lighter fabrics.

Cutting:

Background
1 - 2 ¾" x 21" strip, subcut into:
    1 - 2 ¾" x 3 ½" rectangle (A)

2 - 2 ½" x 21" strips, subcut into:
    1 - 2 ½" x 5 ½" rectangle (B)
    1 - 2 ½" x 4 ¾" rectangle (C)
    1 - 2 ½" x 4 ¼" rectangle (D)
    1 - 2 ½" x 4" rectangle (E)
    1 - 2 ½" x 3 ¾" rectangle (F)
    1 - 2 ½" x 3 ¼" rectangle (G)
    1 - 2 ½" x 3" rectangle (H)

3 - 2" x 21" strips, subcut into:
    1 - 2" x 5" rectangle (I)
    8 - 2" squares (J)
    1 - 1 ¾" x 4 ¼" rectangle (K)
    2 - 1 ¾" x 3 ½" rectangles (L)
    1 - 1 ¾" x 2 ½" rectangle (M)
    1 - 1 ¾" x 2 ¼" rectangle (N)
    2 - 1 ½" x 2 ½" rectangles (O)
    4 - 1 ½" squares (P)

Flowers - from one fabric cut
    4 - 2" squares (Q)

Flowers - from one fabric cut
    4 - 2" squares (Q)
    4 - 1 ½" squares (R)

Flower Accent
    2 - 2" squares (S)
    1 - 1 ½" square (T)

Stems and Leaves
    3 - 2 ½" squares (U)
    1 - 1 ¾" square (V)
    1 - 1" x 8" rectangle (W)
    1 - 1" x 7 ¼" rectangle (X)
    1 - 1" x 6 ½" rectangle (Y)

Leaves
    2 - 2 ½" squares (U)
    2 - 1 ¾" squares (V)

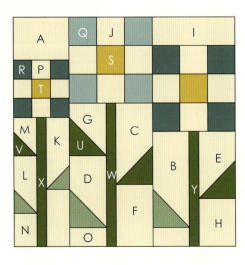

Construction:

1 Assemble four Fabric R squares, four Fabric P squares and the Fabric T square.

Make 1 Small Nine Patch Flower Unit.
3 ½" x 3 ½" unfinished.

2 Assemble four matching Fabric Q squares, four Fabric J squares and one Fabric S square.

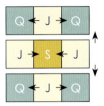 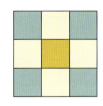

Make 2 Large Nine Patch Flower Units.
5" x 5" unfinished.

3 Draw a diagonal line on the wrong side of the Fabric V squares.

With right sides facing, layer a Fabric V square on the bottom end of the Fabric M rectangle.

Stitch on the drawn line and trim ¼" away from the seam.

Make 1 Fabric M Leaf Unit.
1 ¾" x 2 ½" unfinished.

4 With right sides facing, layer a Fabric V square on the bottom end of a Fabric L rectangle.

Stitch on the drawn line and trim ¼" away from the seam.

Make 1 Fabric L Leaf Unit.
1 ¾" x 3 ½" unfinished.

5 With right sides facing, layer a Fabric V square on the bottom end of the Fabric K rectangle.

Stitch on the drawn line and trim ¼" away from the seam.

Make 1 Fabric K Leaf Unit.
1 ¾" x 4 ¼" unfinished.

6 Assemble the Fabric M Leaf Unit, the Fabric L Leaf Unit, the Fabric N rectangle, the Fabric X rectangle, the Fabric K Leaf Unit and one Fabric L rectangle.

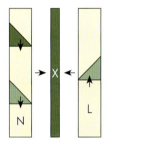 

Make 1 Left Leaf Unit.
3 ½" x 7 ¼" unfinished.

7 Draw a diagonal line on the wrong side of the Fabric U squares.

With right sides facing, layer a Fabric U square on the bottom end of the Fabric G rectangle.

Stitch on the drawn line and trim ¼" away from the seam.

Make 1 Fabric G Leaf Unit.
2 ½" x 3 ¼" unfinished.

NINE PATCH DAISY BLOCK

8   With right sides facing, layer a Fabric U square on the bottom end of the Fabric D rectangle.

Stitch on the drawn line and trim ¼" away from the seam.

Make 1 Fabric D Leaf Unit.
2 ½" x 4 ¼" unfinished.

9   With right sides facing, layer a Fabric U square on the bottom end of the Fabric C rectangle.

Stitch on the drawn line and trim ¼" away from the seam.

Make 1 Fabric C Leaf Unit.
2 ½" x 4 ¾" unfinished.

10   Assemble the Fabric G Leaf Unit, the Fabric D Leaf Unit, one Fabric O rectangle, the Fabric W rectangle, the Fabric C Leaf Unit and the Fabric F rectangle.

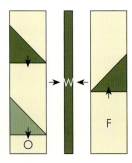 

Make 1 Center Leaf Unit.
5" x 8" unfinished.

11   With right sides facing, layer a Fabric U square on the bottom end of the Fabric B rectangle.

Stitch on the drawn line and trim ¼" away from the seam.

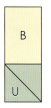 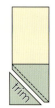 

Make 1 Fabric B Leaf Unit.
2 ½" x 5 ½" unfinished.

12   With right sides facing, layer a Fabric U square on the bottom end of the Fabric E rectangle.

Stitch on the drawn line and trim ¼" away from the seam.

Make 1 Fabric E Leaf Unit.
2 ½" x 4" unfinished.

13   Assemble the Fabric B Leaf Unit, one Fabric O rectangle, the Fabric Y rectangle, the Fabric E Leaf Unit and the Fabric H rectangle.

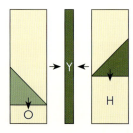 

Make 1 Right Leaf Unit.
5" x 6 ½" unfinished.

14 Assemble the Fabric A rectangle, the Small Nine Patch Flower Unit and the Left Leaf Unit.

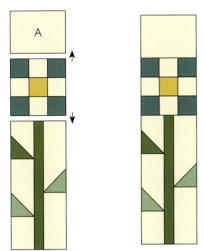

Make 1 Left Nine Patch Daisy Unit.
3 ½" x 12 ½" unfinished.

15 Assemble one Large Nine Patch Flower Unit and the Center Leaf Unit.

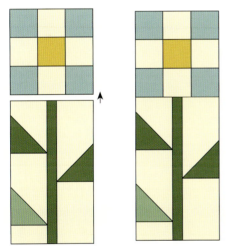

Make 1 Center Nine Patch Daisy Unit.
5" x 12 ½" unfinished.

16 Assemble the Fabric I rectangle, one Large Nine Patch Flower Unit and the Right Leaf Unit.

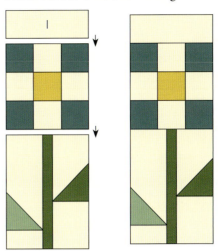

Make 1 Right Nine Patch Daisy Unit.
5" x 12 ½" unfinished.

17 Assemble the Left Nine Patch Daisy Unit, the Center Nine Patch Daisy Unit and the Right Nine Patch Daisy Unit.

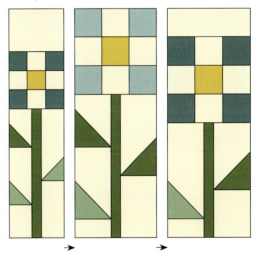

Make 1 Nine Patch Daisy Block.
12 ½" x 12 ½" unfinished.

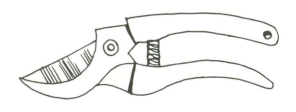

Make 1. 12 ½" x 12 ½" unfinished.

42268-12 42267-32 42264-34 42265-44 42261-42 42261-32

42260-22 42265-34 42262-38 42266-30

Edyta's Tips:

Always press your seams away from the center of the log cabin block.

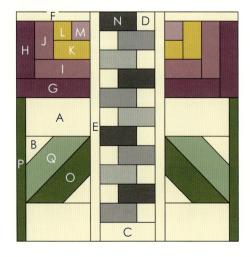

Fabric Requirements:

Background One Fat Quarter (18" x 21")	Fabrics A to F
Flowers Four 10" squares	Fabrics G to M
Sidewalk Three 10" squares	Fabric N
Stems and Leaves One 10" square	Fabrics O & P
Leaves One 10" square	Fabric Q

Cutting:

Background
2 - 2 ½" x 21" strips, subcut into:
    4 - 2 ½" x 4" rectangles (A)
    4 - 2" squares (B)

1 - 1 ½" x 21" strip, subcut into:
    1 - 1 ½" x 3 ½" rectangle (C)
    11 - 1 ½" squares (D)

2 - 1" x 21" strips, subcut into:
    2 - 1" x 12 ½" rectangles (E)
    2 - 1" x 4 ½" rectangles (F)

Flowers - from one fabric cut
    2 - 1 ½" x 4 ½" rectangles (G)
    2 - 1 ½" x 3 ½" rectangles (H)

Flowers - from one fabric cut
    2 - 1 ½" x 3 ½" rectangles (I)
    2 - 1 ½" x 2 ½" rectangles (J)

Flowers - from one fabric cut
    2 - 1 ½" x 2 ½" rectangles (K)
    2 - 1 ½" squares (L)

Flowers - from one fabric cut
    2 - 1 ½" squares (M)

Sidewalk - from each fabric cut
    4 - 1 ½" x 2 ½" rectangles (N)

Stems and Leaves
    1 - 4 ⅜" square (O)
    2 - 1" x 8" rectangles (P)

Leaves
    1 - 4 ⅜" square (Q)

Construction:

1 Assemble one Fabric L square, one Fabric M square and one Fabric K rectangle.

Make 2 Log Cabin Rose One Units.
2 ½" x 2 ½" unfinished.

2 Assemble one Fabric J rectangle, one Log Cabin Rose One Unit and one Fabric I rectangle.

Make 2 Log Cabin Rose Two Units.
3 ½" x 3 ½" unfinished.

3 Assemble one Fabric H rectangle, one Log Cabin Rose Two Unit and one Fabric G rectangle.

Make 2 Log Cabin Rose Units.
4 ½" x 4 ½" unfinished.

4 Draw a diagonal line on the wrong side of the Fabric Q square.

With right sides facing, layer the Fabric Q square with the Fabric O square.

Stitch ¼" from each side of the drawn line.

Cut apart on the marked line.

Make 2 Half Square Triangle Units.
4" x 4" unfinished.

5 Draw a diagonal line on the wrong side of the Fabric B squares.

With right sides facing, layer a Fabric B square on the top left corner of a Half Square Triangle Unit.

Stitch on the drawn line and trim ¼" away from the seam.

Repeat on the bottom right corner.

Make 2 Leaf Units.
4" x 4" unfinished.

6 Assemble two Fabric A rectangles, one Leaf Unit and one Fabric P rectangle.

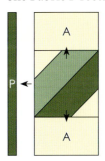 

Make 1 Partial Left Rose Unit.
4 ½" x 8" unfinished.

7 Assemble two Fabric A rectangles, one Leaf Unit and one Fabric P rectangle.

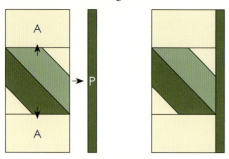

Make 1 Partial Right Rose Unit.
4 ½" x 8" unfinished.

8 Assemble one Fabric F rectangle, one Log Cabin Rose Unit and the Partial Left Rose Unit.

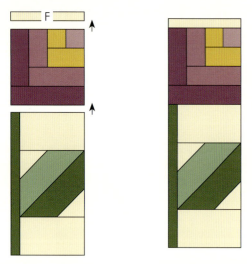

Make 1 Left Rose Unit.
4 ½" x 12 ½" unfinished.

9 Assemble one Fabric F rectangle, one Log Cabin Rose Unit and the Partial Right Rose Unit.

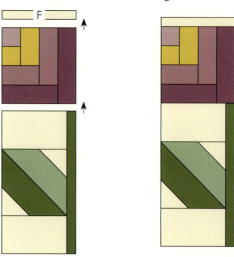

Make 1 Right Rose Unit.
4 ½" x 12 ½" unfinished.

10 Assemble eleven Fabric N rectangles, eleven Fabric D squares and the Fabric C rectangle.

One of the Fabric N rectangles will not be used.

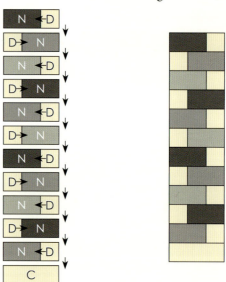

Make 1 Sidewalk Unit.
3 ½" x 12 ½" unfinished.

11 Assemble the Left Rose Unit, two Fabric E rectangles, the Sidewalk Unit and the Right Rose Unit.

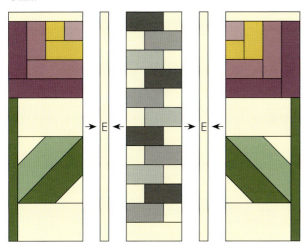

E ← → E

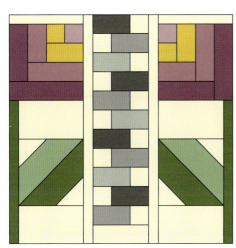

Make 1 Sidewalk and Log Cabin Roses Block.
12 ½" x 12 ½" unfinished.

Make 1. 12 ½" x 12 ½" unfinished.

42260-12   42264-41   42265-40   42268-46   42268-50   42262-38

42265-27   42266-30

Edyta's Tips:

When piecing the Petunia Petal Units, be careful not to pull or stretch the bias edges.

Fabric Requirements:

Background One Fat Quarter (18" x 21")	Fabrics A to L
Flowers Three 10" squares	Fabric M
Flower Accent One 10" square	Fabric N
Stems and Leaves Two 10" squares	Fabrics O to R
Stem One 10" square	Fabric S

Cutting:

Background
2 - 3 ¼" x 21" strips, subcut into:
   3 - 3 ¼" squares (A) *Cut each on the diagonal twice*
   1 - 2 ½" x 4 ½" rectangle (B)
   1 - 2 ¼" x 3 ¾" rectangle (C)
   3 - 2 ¼" x 3" rectangles (D)

1 - 2 ¼" x 21" strip, subcut into:
   1 - 2 ¼" x 2 ½" rectangle (E)
   4 - 2 ¼" squares (F)
   3 - 2" x 2 ¼" rectangles (G)

1 - 1 ¾" x 21" strip, subcut into:
   1 - 1 ¾" x 2 ¼" rectangle (H)
   1 - 1 ½" x 2 ¼" rectangle (I)

2 - 1 ¼" x 21" strips, subcut into:
   1 - 1 ¼" x 2 ¼" rectangle (J)
   18 - 1 ¼" x 1 ½" rectangles (K)
   1 - 1" x 4 ½" rectangle (L)

Flowers - from each fabric cut
   2 - 2 ⅞" squares (M) *Cut each on the diagonal once*

Flower Accent
   3 - 3 ¼" squares (N) *Cut each on the diagonal twice*

Stems and Leaves - from one fabric cut
   4 - 1 ½" squares (O)
   4 - 1 ¼" squares (P)
   1 - 1" x 8" rectangle (Q)

Stems and Leaves - from one fabric cut
   5 - 1 ½" squares (O)
   5 - 1 ¼" squares (P)
   1 - 1" x 8 ½" rectangle (R)

Stem
   1 - 1" x 6 ½" rectangle (S)

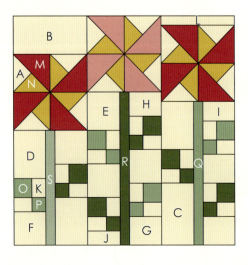

Construction:

1 Assemble one Fabric A triangle, one Fabric N triangle and one Fabric M triangle.

Make 12 Petunia Petal Units.
2 ½" x 2 ½" unfinished.

2 Assemble four matching Petunia Petal Units.

Make 3 Petunia Flower Units.
4 ½" x 4 ½" unfinished.

3 Assemble one Fabric O square, two Fabric K rectangles and one matching Fabric P square.

Make 9 Petunia Leaf Units.
2 ¼" x 2 ¼" unfinished.

4 Assemble two Fabric D rectangles, two different Petunia Leaf Units, two Fabric F squares and the Fabric S rectangle.

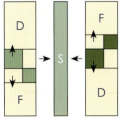 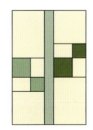

Make 1 Partial Left Petunia Unit.
4 ½" x 6 ½" unfinished.

5 Assemble the Fabric B rectangle, one Petunia Flower Unit and the Partial Left Petunia Unit.

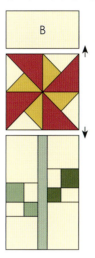 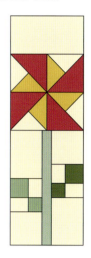

Make 1 Left Petunia Unit.
4 ½" x 12 ½" unfinished.

6 Assemble the Fabric E rectangle, two matching Petunia Leaf Units, two Fabric F squares, two different matching Petunia Leaf Units, the Fabric J rectangle, the Fabric R rectangle, the Fabric H rectangle and one Fabric G rectangle.

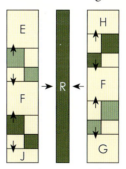 

Make 1 Partial Center Petunia Unit.
4 ½" x 8 ½" unfinished.

7 Assemble one Petunia Flower Unit and the Partial Center Petunia Unit.

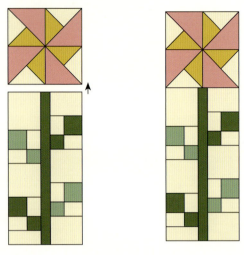

Make 1 Center Petunia Unit.
4 ½" x 12 ½" unfinished.

8 Assemble one Fabric D rectangle, two matching Petunia Leaf Units, the Fabric C rectangle, the Fabric Q rectangle, the Fabric I rectangle, one different Petunia Leaf Unit and two Fabric G rectangles.

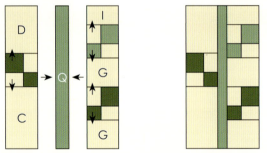

Make 1 Partial Right Petunia Unit.
4 ½" x 8" unfinished.

9 Assemble the Fabric L rectangle, one Petunia Flower Unit and the Partial Right Petunia Unit.

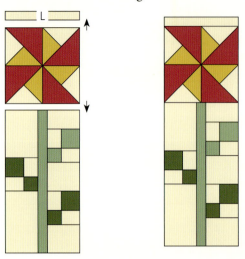

Make 1 Right Petunia Unit.
4 ½" x 12 ½" unfinished.

10 Assemble the Left Petunia Unit, the Center Petunia Unit and the Right Petunia Unit.

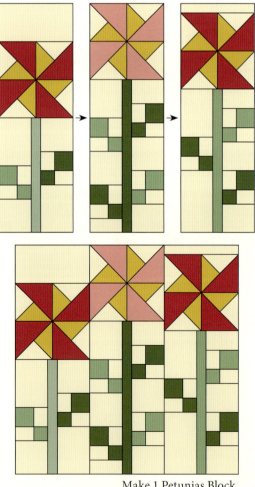

Make 1 Petunias Block.
12 ½" x 12 ½" unfinished.

Make 1. 12 ½" x 12 ½" unfinished.

42260-12   42264-41   42261-42   42268-50   42261-38   42266-30

Fabric Requirements:

Background	Fabrics A to G
One Fat Quarter (18" x 21")	
Flowers	Fabrics H, I & J
Three Fat Eighths (9" x 21")	
Stems and Leaves	Fabrics K to N
One Fat Eighth (9" x 21")	
Leaves	Fabric O
One 10" x 10" square	

Edyta's Tips:

Don't be afraid to mix and match your prints to make the tulips in this block. Little splashes of color can make a block beautiful!

Cutting:

Background

1 - 3" x 21" strip, subcut into:
    2 - 3" squares (A) *Cut each on the diagonal twice* *
    3 - 2 ⅝" squares (B) *Cut each on the diagonal once*

2 - 2" x 21" strips, subcut into:
    4 - 2" x 3 ½" rectangles (C)
    4 - 2" x 2 ⅞" rectangles (D)
    4 - 2" x 2 ¾" rectangles (E)

3 - 1" x 21" strips, subcut into:
    3 - 1" x 12 ½" rectangles (F)
    1 - 1" x 4" rectangle (G)

Flowers - from each fabric cut
    1 - 4 ¾" square (H) *Cut on the diagonal twice* *
    1 - 4 ⅜" square (I) *Cut on the diagonal once* *
    1 - 1 ¾" square (J)

Stems and Leaves
    1 - 4 ¾" square (K) *Cut on the diagonal twice* *
    3 - 2" x 5" rectangles (L)
    2 - 1" x 7 ¼" rectangles (M)
    1 - 1" x 6 ¾" rectangle (N)

Leaves
    3 - 2" x 5" rectangles (O)

* *Not all of the Fabric A triangles, Fabric H triangles, Fabric I triangles and Fabric K triangles will be used.*

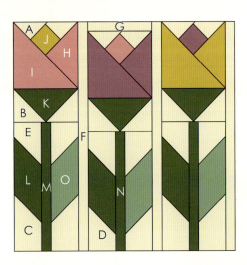

Construction:

1 Assemble two Fabric A triangles and one Fabric J square.

Make 3 Partial Flower Units.

2 Assemble one Partial Flower Unit, one Fabric H triangle and one matching Fabric I triangle.

Make 3 Flower Units.
4" x 4" unfinished.

3 Assemble two Fabric B triangles and one Fabric K triangle.

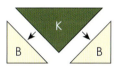

Make 3 Flying Geese Units.
2 ¼" x 4" unfinished.

4 On the wrong side of the Fabric L rectangles, mark a dot 2" over from the top right corner. Draw a line from the bottom right corner to the dot.

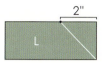

With right sides facing, layer a marked Fabric L rectangle with a Fabric C rectangle. Stitch on the drawn line and trim ¼" away from the seam.

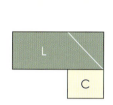  

Make 2 Partial Left Large Leaf Units.
2" x 6 ½" unfinished.

5 On the wrong side of two Fabric E rectangles, mark a dot 2" over from the top right corner. Draw a line from the bottom right corner to the dot.

With right sides facing, layer a marked Fabric E rectangle with a Partial Left Large Leaf Unit. Stitch on the drawn line and trim ¼" away from the seam.

Make 2 Left Large Leaf Units.
2" x 7 ¼" unfinished.

6 With right sides facing, layer a marked Fabric L rectangle with a Fabric D rectangle. Stitch on the drawn line and trim ¼" away from the seam.

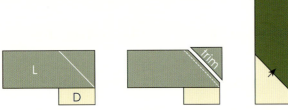

Make 1 Partial Left Small Leaf Unit.
2" x 5 ⅞" unfinished.

7 On the wrong side of one Fabric D rectangle, mark a dot 2" over from the top right corner. Draw a line from the bottom right corner to the dot.

With right sides facing, layer the marked Fabric D rectangle with the Partial Left Small Leaf Unit. Stitch on the drawn line and trim ¼" away from the seam.

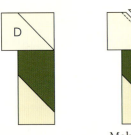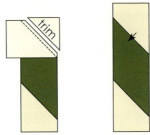

Make 1 Left Small Leaf Unit.
2" x 6 ¾" unfinished.

8 On the wrong side of the Fabric O rectangles, mark a dot 2" over from the top left corner. Draw a line from the bottom left corner to the dot.

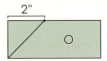

With right sides facing, layer a marked Fabric O rectangle with a Fabric C rectangle. Stitch on the drawn line and trim ¼" away from the seam.

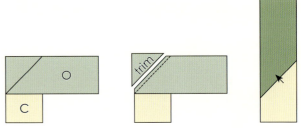

Make 2 Partial Right Large Leaf Units.
2" x 6 ½" unfinished.

9 On the wrong side of the remaining Fabric E rectangles, mark a dot 2" over from the top left corner. Draw a line from the bottom left corner to the dot.

With right sides facing, layer a marked Fabric E rectangle with a Partial Right Large Leaf Unit. Stitch on the drawn line and trim ¼" away from the seam.

Make 2 Right Large Leaf Units.
2" x 7 ¼" unfinished.

10 With right sides facing, layer a marked Fabric O rectangle with a Fabric D rectangle. Stitch on the drawn line and trim ¼" away from the seam.

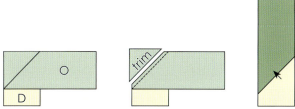

Make 1 Partial Right Small Leaf Unit.
2" x 5 ⅞" unfinished.

11 On the wrong side of the remaining Fabric D rectangle, mark a dot 2" over from the top left corner. Draw a line from the bottom left corner to the dot.

With right sides facing, layer the marked Fabric D rectangle with the Partial Right Small Leaf Unit. Stitch on the drawn line and trim ¼" away from the seam.

Make 1 Right Small Leaf Unit.
2" x 6 ¾" unfinished.

12 Assemble one Flower Unit, one Flying Geese Unit, one Left Large Leaf Unit, one Fabric M rectangle and one Right Large Leaf Unit.

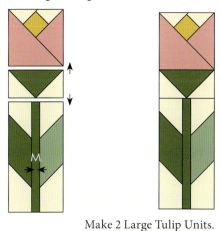

Make 2 Large Tulip Units.
4" x 12 ½" unfinished.

13 Assemble the Fabric G rectangle, one Flower Unit, one Flying Geese Unit, the Left Small Leaf Unit, the Fabric N rectangle and the Right Small Leaf Unit.

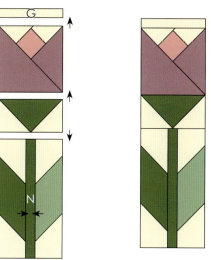

Make 1 Small Tulip Unit.
4" x 12 ½" unfinished.

14 Assemble two Large Tulip Units, three Fabric F rectangles, and the Small Tulip Unit.

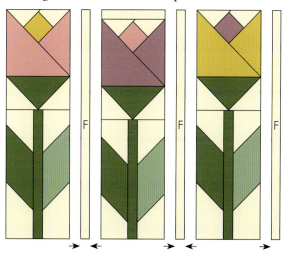

Make 1 Tulips Block.
12 ½" x 12 ½" unfinished.

Make 1. 12 ½" x 12 ½" unfinished.

42268-12   42264-41   42268-46   42268-50   42266-30   42261-38

Edyta's Tips:

I added leaves to this block by simply cutting apart the background rectangles and then sewing them back together with 1" green strips in between. As long as the strips are 1" wide, the background rectangles will remain the same size. You can use this technique to easily add a strip of color to any background.

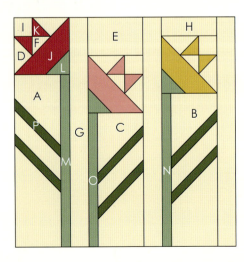

Fabric Requirements:

Background One Fat Quarter (18" x 21")	Fabrics A to I
Flowers Three 10" squares	Fabrics J & K
Stems One 10" square	Fabrics L to O
Leaves One 10" square	Fabric P

Cutting:

Background
2 - 4" x 21" strips, subcut into:
    1 - 4" x 10 ½" rectangle (A)
    1 - 4" x 9 ½" rectangle (B)
    1 - 4" x 8 ½" rectangle (C)
    2 - 3 ¼" squares (D) *Cut each on the diagonal twice* *
    1 - 2 ½" x 3 ½" rectangle (E)

1 - 1 ⅞" x 21" strip, subcut into:
    2 - 1 ⅞" squares (F) *Cut each on the diagonal once* *

3 - 1 ½" x 21" strips, subcut into:
    3 - 1 ½" x 12 ½" rectangles (G)
    1 - 1 ½" x 3 ½" rectangle (H)
    3 - 1 ½" squares (I)

Flowers - from each fabric cut
    1 - 3 ⅞" square (J) *Cut each on the diagonal once* *
    1 - 1 ⅞" square (K) *Cut each on the diagonal once*

Stems
    3 - 1 ½" squares (L)
    1 - 1" x 9 ½" rectangle (M)
    1 - 1" x 8 ½" rectangle (N)
    1 - 1" x 7 ½" rectangle (O)

Leaves
    6 - 1" x 7" rectangles (P)

* *Not all of the Fabric D triangles, Fabric F triangles and Fabric J triangles will be used.*

Construction:

1   Assemble one Fabric I square, two Fabric K triangles and one Fabric F triangle.

Make 3 Top Left Flower Units.

2   Assemble two Fabric D triangles and one Top Left Flower Unit.

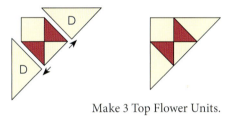

Make 3 Top Flower Units.

3   Assemble one Top Flower Unit and one matching Fabric J triangle.

Make 3 Partial Flower Units.
3 ½" x 3 ½" unfinished.

4   Draw a diagonal line on the wrong side of the Fabric L squares.

With right sides facing, layer a Fabric L square on the bottom right corner of a Partial Flower Unit.

Stitch on the drawn line and trim ¼" away from the seam.

Make 3 Flower Units.
3 ½" x 3 ½" unfinished.

5   Mark 1 ½" and 3" down from the top left corner of the Fabric A rectangle. Align the 45° line on your ruler with the marks and cut.

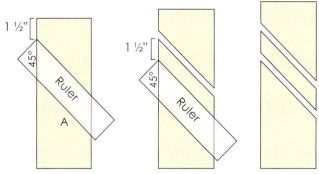

Make 1 Partial Left Leaf Unit.

6   Assemble the Partial Left Leaf Unit and two Fabric P rectangles.

Trim Left Leaf Unit to measure 3" x 9 ½".

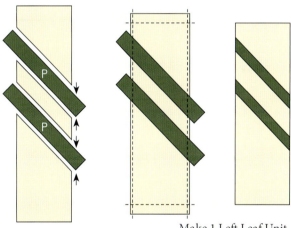

Make 1 Left Leaf Unit.
3" x 9 ½" unfinished.

7   Mark 1 ½" and 3" down from the top right corner of the Fabric C rectangle. Align the 45° line on your ruler with the marks and cut.

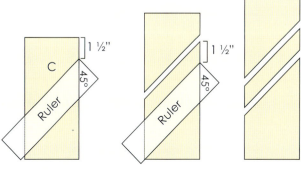

Make 1 Partial Center Leaf Unit.

8 Assemble the Partial Center Leaf Unit and two Fabric P rectangles.

Trim Center Leaf Unit to measure 3" x 7 ½".

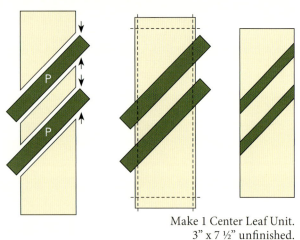

Make 1 Center Leaf Unit.
3" x 7 ½" unfinished.

9 Mark 1 ½" and 3" down from the top right corner of the Fabric B rectangle. Align the 45° line on your ruler with the marks and cut.

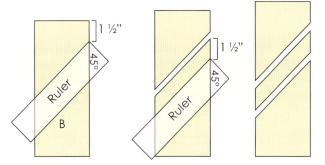

Make 1 Partial Right Leaf Unit.

10 Assemble the Partial Right Leaf Unit and two Fabric P rectangles.

Trim Right Leaf Unit to measure 3" x 8 ½".

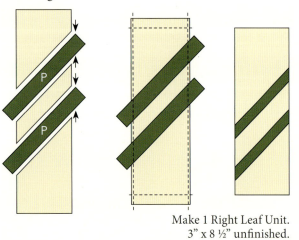

Make 1 Right Leaf Unit.
3" x 8 ½" unfinished.

11 Assemble one Flower Unit, the Left Leaf Unit and the Fabric M rectangle.

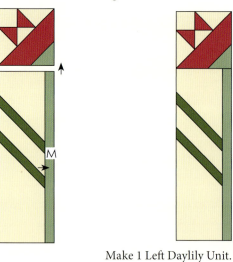

Make 1 Left Daylily Unit.
3 ½" x 12 ½" unfinished.

12 Assemble the Fabric E rectangle, one Flower Unit, the Fabric O rectangle and the Center Leaf Unit.

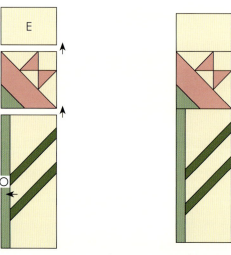

Make 1 Center Daylily Unit.
3 ½" x 12 ½" unfinished.

13 Assemble the Fabric H rectangle, one Flower Unit, the Fabric N rectangle and the Right Leaf Unit.

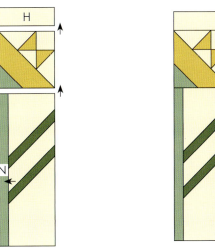

Make 1 Right Daylily Unit.
3 ½" x 12 ½" unfinished.

14 Assemble the Left Daylily Unit, three Fabric G rectangles, the Center Daylily Unit and the Right Daylily Unit.

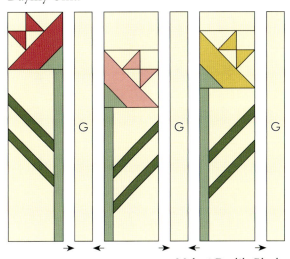

Make 1 Daylily Block.
12 ½" x 12 ½" unfinished.

DAHLIA BLOCK

Make 1. 12 ½" x 12 ½" unfinished.

42266-12 42264-34 42261-42 42267-32 42268-50 42261-38

42266-30

Edyta's Tips:

To secure your fabrics to the hexagon paper, you can either baste the fabric in place or use a touch of glue.

Fabric Requirements:

Background	Fabrics A to I
One Fat Quarter (18" x 21")	
Flowers	Fabric J
Three 10" squares	
Flower Accent	Fabric K
One 10" square	
Stems and Leaves	Fabrics L & M
Two 10" x 15" rectangles	
Cardstock Paper	
One 8 ½" x 11" sheet	

Cutting:

Background

1 - 5" x 21" strip, subcut into:
    1 - 5" x 12 ½" rectangle (A)
    1 - 3 ¼" x 4 ¾" rectangle (B)

1 - 2 ¾" x 21" strip, subcut into:
    2 - 2 ¾" x 4 ¾" rectangles (C)
    1 - 2 ½" x 3 ¾" rectangle (D)

1 - 1 ½" x 21" strip, subcut into:
    1 - 1 ½" x 3 ¾" rectangle (E)
    1 - 1 ½" x 3 ¼" rectangle (F)
    4 - 1 ½" x 2 ¾" rectangles (G)

1 - 1 ¼" x 21" strip, subcut into:
    10 - 1 ¼" squares (H)
    1 - 1" x 2 ¾" rectangle (I)

Flowers - from each fabric cut
    6 - Flower Hexagon Units (J) *See page 37*

Flower Accent
    3 - Center Hexagon Units (K) *See page 37*

Stems and Leaves - from one fabric cut
    4 - 2 ¾" squares (L)
    2 - 1" x 8" rectangles (M)

Stems and Leaves - from one fabric cut
    1 - 2 ¾" square (L)
    1 - 1" x 8" rectangle (M)

¾" Hexagon Template and ¾" Paper Template
    Templates are on page 108.

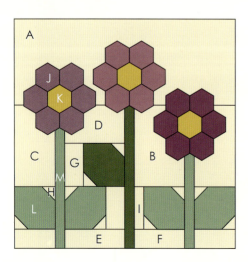

Construction:

1 Using the ¾" Hexagon Template, cut six Fabric J Hexagon Units from each Fabric J square and cut three Fabric K Hexagon Units from the Fabric K square.

Make 18
Flower Hexagon Units.

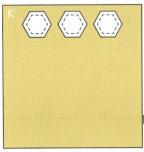

Make 3
Flower Accent Hexagon Units.

2 Using the ¾" Paper Template, cut twenty-one Paper Hexagon Units using cardstock paper.

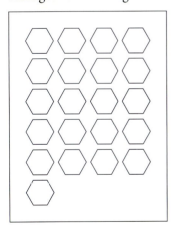

Make 21
Paper Hexagon Units.

3 Place one Paper Hexagon Unit in the center of the wrong side of one Flower Hexagon Unit.

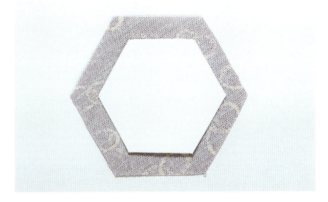

4 Fold the fabric around the edge of the template and fold each corner in the same direction.

Secure fabric around the edge of the paper template with a needle and thread using a basting stitch. Do not stitch through the paper template. All edges of the paper template need to be covered.

Stitch twice at the end to lock the stitch. Remember not to make it too tight since you will be removing the basting stitches later.

5 Place two hexagons right sides together.

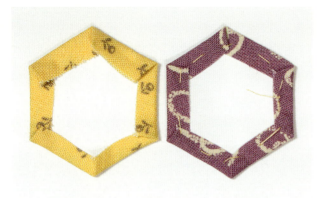

6 Using piecing thread, slip your needle under the seam allowance in the corner. Shorter thread is easier to work with. Remember to put a knot in the end.

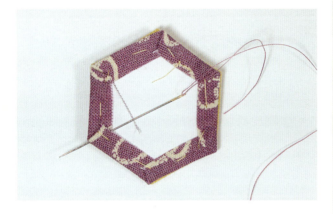

7 Start with a double stitch at the point to lock the stitches. Stitch along one edge with a whip stitch. Remember to stitch only through the fabric, not the paper.

8 Finish the seam with a double stitch and do not cut the thread. Open the shapes.

9 Add another fabric shape and place fabric right sides together with your previously sewn unit.

10 Start with a double stitch to lock the stitches. Stitch along one edge of the additional shape with a whip stitch.

11 Finish the seam with a double stitch and do not cut the thread. Open the shape then move on to stitching the next open seam.

12 Fold the previously sewn shapes in half if necessary while sewing the next seam.

13 Proceed in adding the rest of the hexagons.

Carefully remove the basting stitches and the paper.

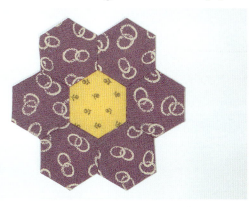

Make 3 Hexagon Flower Units.

DAHLIA BLOCK

14 Draw a diagonal line on the wrong side of the Fabric H squares.

With right sides facing, layer a Fabric H square on the top right corner of a Fabric L square.

Stitch on the drawn line and trim ¼" away from the seam.

Repeat on the bottom left corner.

Make 5 Leaf Units.
2 ¾" x 2 ¾" unfinished.

15 Assemble one Fabric C rectangle, one Leaf Unit and one Fabric G rectangle.

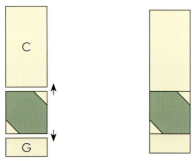

Make 1 Far Left Stem Unit.
2 ¾" x 8" unfinished.

16 Assemble the Fabric D rectangle, two Fabric G rectangles, two different Leaf Units and the Fabric E rectangle.

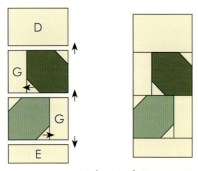

Make 1 Left Stem Unit.
3 ¾" x 8" unfinished.

17 Assemble the Fabric B rectangle, the Fabric I rectangle, one Leaf Unit and the Fabric F rectangle.

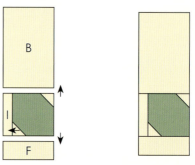

Make 1 Right Stem Unit.
3 ¼" x 8" unfinished.

18 Assemble one Fabric C rectangle, one Leaf Unit and one Fabric G rectangle.

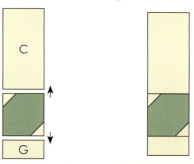

Make 1 Far Right Stem Unit.
2 ¾" x 8" unfinished.

19 Assemble the Far Left Stem Unit, three Fabric M rectangles, the Left Stem Unit, the Right Stem Unit and the Far Right Stem Unit.

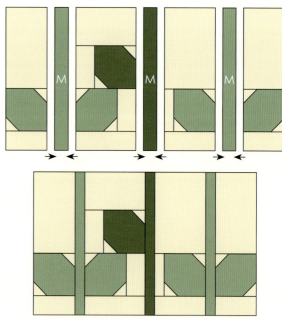

Make 1 Bottom Dahlia Unit.
8" x 12 ½" unfinished.

20 Assemble the Fabric A rectangle and the Bottom Dahlia Unit.

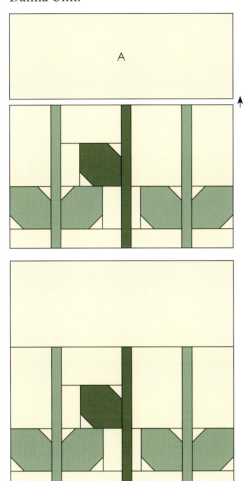

Make 1 Partial Dahlia Unit.
12 ½" x 12 ½" unfinished.

21 Using your applique method of choice, applique the Hexagon Flower Units to the Partial Dahlia Unit.

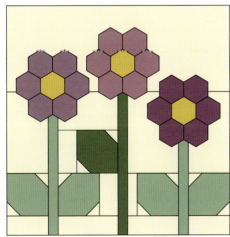

Make 1 Dahlia Block.
12 ½" x 12 ½" unfinished.

Make 1. 12 ½" x 12 ½" unfinished.

42260-12   42266-12   42267-12   42268-12   42264-34   42261-42

42268-44   42266-30   42261-38

Edyta's Tips:

When cutting a 60° triangle, notice that two sides of the triangle will be bias and one will be on the straight of grain. Pay attention to the straight of grain side and position it horizontally in the block so the fabrics will lie nice and flat.

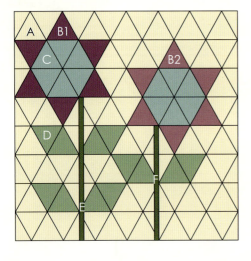

Fabric Requirements:

Background Four 10" squares	Fabric A
Flowers Two 10" squares	Fabric B
Flower Accent One 10" square	Fabric C
Leaves One 10" square	Fabric D
Stems One 10" square	Fabrics E & F
½" Bias Tape Maker	

Cutting:

Background - from each fabric cut
    4 - 2 ¼" x 10" rectangles (A)

Flowers - from each fabric cut
    1 - 2 ¼" x 10" rectangle (B)

Flower Accent
    2 - 2 ¼" x 10" rectangles (C)

Leaves
    2 - 2 ¼" x 10" rectangles (D)

Stems
    1 - 1" x 8" rectangle (E)
    1 - 1" x 6 ½" rectangle (F)

60° Triangle Template
    Template is on page 108.

Construction:

1 Using the 60° Triangle Template, cut eighty-four Fabric A triangles from the Fabric A rectangles, cut six Fabric B triangles from each Fabric B rectangle, cut six Fabric C triangles from each Fabric C rectangle and cut six Fabric D triangles from each Fabric D rectangle.

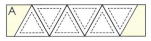

Make 84 total Fabric A Triangle Units.

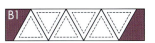

Make 6 Fabric B1 Triangle Units.

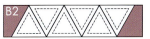

Make 6 Fabric B2 Triangle Units.

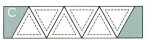

Make 12 Fabric C Triangle Units.

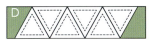

Make 12 Fabric D Triangle Units.

2 Assemble fourteen Fabric A Triangle Units and one Fabric B1 Triangle Unit. Press open.

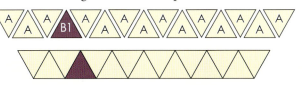

Make 1 Honeysuckle Row One.

3 Assemble nine Fabric A Triangle Units, two Fabric B1 Triangle Units, three Fabric C Triangle Units and one Fabric B2 Triangle Unit. Press open.

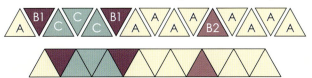

Make 1 Honeysuckle Row Two.

4 Assemble five Fabric A Triangle Units, two Fabric B1 Triangle Units, six Fabric C Triangle Units and two Fabric B2 Triangle Units. Press open.

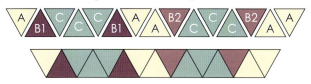

Make 1 Honeysuckle Row Three.

5 Assemble nine Fabric A Triangle Units, one Fabric B1 Triangle Unit, two Fabric B2 Triangle Units and three Fabric C Triangle Units. Press open.

Make 1 Honeysuckle Row Four.

6 Assemble ten Fabric A Triangle Units, four Fabric D Triangle Units and one Fabric B2 Triangle Unit. Press open.

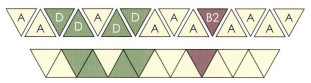

Make 1 Honeysuckle Row Five.

7 Assemble eleven Fabric A Triangle Units and four Fabric D Triangle Units. Press open.

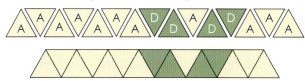

Make 1 Honeysuckle Row Six.

8 Assemble eleven Fabric A Triangle Units and four Fabric D Triangle Units. Press open.

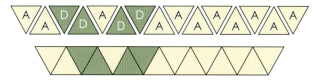

Make 1 Honeysuckle Row Seven.

9 Assemble fifteen Fabric A Triangle Units. Press open.

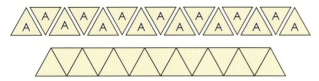

Make 1 Honeysuckle Row Eight.

10 Assemble the Honeysuckle Row One, the Honeysuckle Row Two and the Honeysuckle Row Three. Press open.

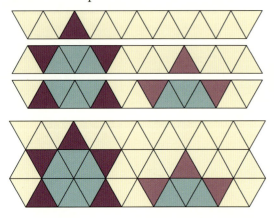

Make 1 Top Honeysuckle Unit.

11 Assemble the Honeysuckle Row Five, the Honeysuckle Row Six, the Honeysuckle Row Seven and the Honeysuckle Row Eight. Press open.

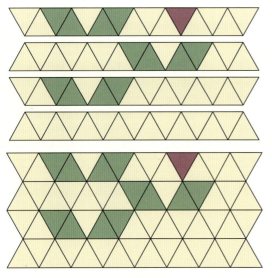

Make 1 Partial Bottom Honeysuckle Unit.

12 Using a ½" bias tape maker, prepare the Fabric E rectangle and the Fabric F rectangle.

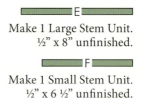

Make 1 Large Stem Unit.
½" x 8" unfinished.

Make 1 Small Stem Unit.
½" x 6 ½" unfinished.

13 Using your applique method of choice, applique the Small Stem Unit to the Partial Bottom Honeysuckle Unit.

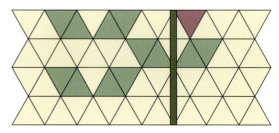

Make 1 Bottom Honeysuckle Unit.

14 Assemble the Honeysuckle Row Four and the Bottom Honeysuckle Unit. Press open.

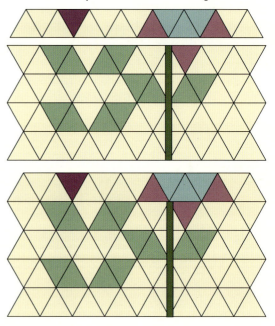

Make 1 Partial Middle Honeysuckle Unit.

15 Using your applique method of choice, applique the Large Stem Unit to the Partial Middle Honeysuckle Unit.

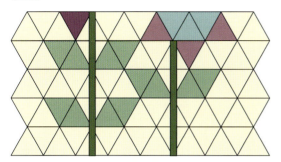

Make 1 Middle Honeysuckle Unit.

16 Assemble the Top Honeysuckle Unit and the Middle Honeysuckle Unit. Press open.

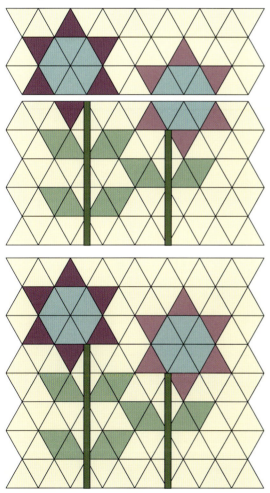

Make 1 Partial Honeysuckle Block Unit.

17 Using a Creative Grids 12 ½" Square It Up Ruler, trim block to measure 12 ½" x 12 ½". Trim ¼" away from the flower points on the left side.

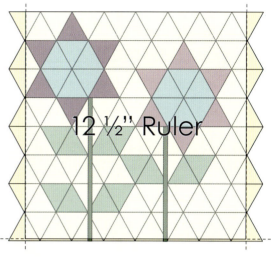

12 ½" Ruler

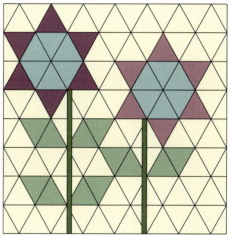

Make 1 Honeysuckle Block.
12 ½" x 12 ½" unfinished.

Make 1. 12 ½" x 12 ½" unfinished.

42267-12

42265-44

42268-44

42261-42

42267-32

42261-38

42266-30

Edyta's Tips:

When cutting diamonds, position the 45° line on your ruler along the edge of your fabric.

Make sure you use pins at seam intersections to keep the bias edges from stretching.

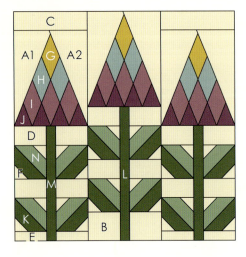

Fabric Requirements:

Background	Fabrics A to F
One Fat Quarter (18" x 21")	
Flowers	Fabrics G to J
Four 10" squares	
Stems and Leaves	Fabrics K, L & M
One 10" x 20" rectangle	
Leaves	Fabric N
One 10" square	

Cutting:

Background

1 - 6 ½" x 21" strip, subcut into:
    2 - 6 ½" x 9 ½" rectangles (A)

2 - 2 ¼" x 21" strips, subcut into:
    2 - 2" x 2 ¼" rectangles (B)
    2 - 1 ½" x 4 ½" rectangles (C)
    12 - 1 ½" x 2 ¼" rectangles (D)
    4 - 1" x 2 ¼" rectangles (E)

2 - 1 ¼" x 21" strips, subcut into:
    24 - 1 ¼" squares (F)

Flowers - from one fabric cut
    1 - 1 ½" x 10" rectangle (G)

Flowers - from one fabric cut
    2 - 1 ½" x 10" rectangles (H)

Flowers - from one fabric cut
    3 - 1 ½" x 10" rectangles (I)

Flowers - from one fabric cut
    4 - 1 ½" x 10" rectangles (J)

Stems and Leaves
    6 - 2 ⅝" squares (K)
    1 - 1" x 7 ½" rectangle (L)
    2 - 1" x 6 ½" rectangles (M)

Leaves
    6 - 2 ⅝" squares (N)

Coneflower Background Template
    Template is on page 108.

Construction:

1 Assemble the Fabric G rectangle, one Fabric H rectangle, one Fabric I rectangle and one Fabric J rectangle. Offset each rectangle about 1" to reduce waste.

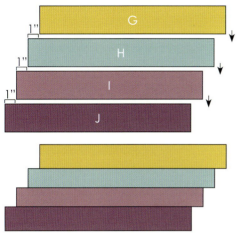

Make 1 Coneflower One Strip Set.
4 ½" x 10" unfinished.

2 Align the 45° line on your ruler with the top edge and trim off the left edge of the Coneflower One Strip Set.

Cut three 1 ½" wide units from the Coneflower One Strip Set.

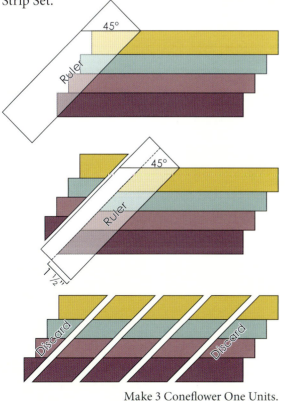

Make 3 Coneflower One Units.

3 Assemble one Fabric H rectangle, one Fabric I rectangle and one Fabric J rectangle. Offset each rectangle about 1" to reduce waste.

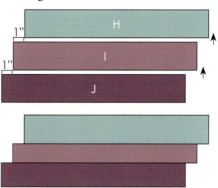

Make 1 Coneflower Two Strip Set.
3 ½" x 10" unfinished.

4 Align the 45° line on your ruler with the top edge and trim off the left edge of the Coneflower Two Strip Set.

Cut three 1 ½" wide units from the Coneflower Two Strip Set.

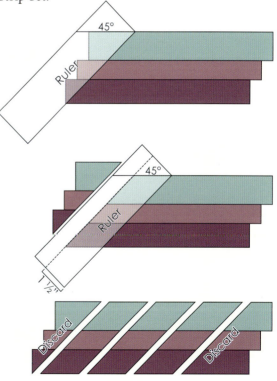

Make 3 Coneflower Two Units.

5   Assemble one Fabric I rectangle and one Fabric J rectangle. Offset each rectangle about 1" to reduce waste.

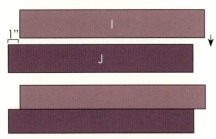

Make 1 Coneflower Three Strip Set.
2 ½" x 10" unfinished.

6   Align the 45° line on your ruler with the top edge and trim off the left edge of the Coneflower Three Strip Set.

Cut three 1 ½" wide units from the Coneflower Three Strip Set.

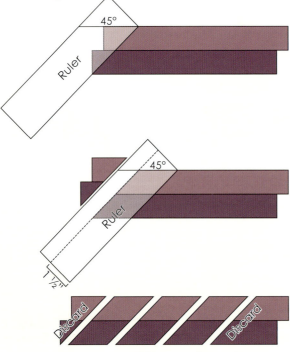

Make 3 Coneflower Three Units.

7   Align the 45° line on your ruler with the top edge and trim off the left edge of a Fabric J rectangle.

Cut three 1 ½" wide units from the Fabric J rectangle.

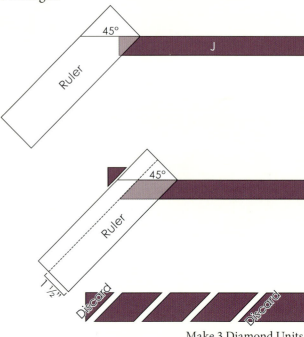

Make 3 Diamond Units.

8   Matching seams, assemble one Coneflower One Unit, one Coneflower Two Unit, one Coneflower Three Unit and one Diamond Unit.

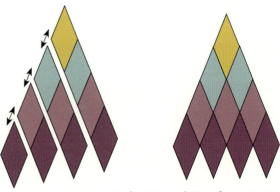

Make 3 Partial Coneflower Units.

9 With right sides facing, layer two Fabric A rectangles.

Using the Coneflower Background Template, cut six Fabric A triangles.

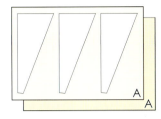

Make 3 Left Side Units.   Make 3 Right Side Units.

10 Assemble one Left Side Unit, one Partial Coneflower Unit and one Right Side Unit.

Trim Coneflower Unit to measure 4 ½" x 5 ½".

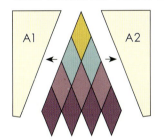

Make 3 Coneflower Units.
4 ½" x 5 ½" unfinished.

11 Draw a diagonal line on the wrong side of the Fabric N squares.

With right sides facing, layer a Fabric N square with a Fabric K square.

Stitch ¼" from each side of the drawn line.

Cut apart on the marked line.

Make 12 Half Square Triangle Units.
2 ¼" x 2 ¼" unfinished.

12 Draw a diagonal line on the wrong side of the Fabric F squares.

With right sides facing, layer a Fabric F square on the bottom left corner of a Half Square Triangle Unit.

Stitch on the drawn line and trim ¼" away from the seam.

Repeat on the top right corner.

Make 12 Leaf Units.
2 ¼" x 2 ¼" unfinished.

13 Assemble four Fabric D rectangles, four Leaf Units, two Fabric E rectangles and one Fabric M rectangle.

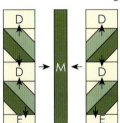

Make 2 Side Stem Units.
4 ½" x 6 ½" unfinished.

14 Assemble one Fabric C rectangle, one Coneflower Unit and one Side Stem Unit.

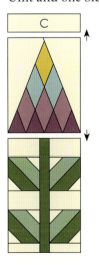

Make 2 Side Flower Units.
4 ½" x 12 ½" unfinished.

15 Assemble four Fabric D rectangles, four Leaf Units, two Fabric B rectangles and the Fabric L rectangle.

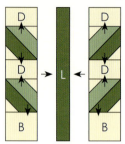 

Make 1 Center Stem Unit.
4 ½" x 7 ½" unfinished.

16 Assemble one Coneflower Unit and the Center Stem Unit.

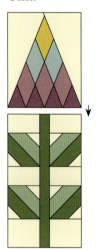 

Make 1 Center Flower Unit.
4 ½" x 12 ½" unfinished.

17 Assemble two Side Flower Units and the Center Flower Unit.

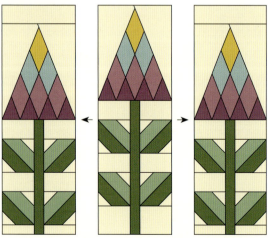

Make 1 Coneflower Block.
12 ½" x 12 ½" unfinished.

Moon Flower Block

Make 1. 12 ½" x 12 ½" unfinished.

 42268-12
 42261-37
42265-44
 42260-31
 42268-44
42266-30

 42265-27
42261-38

Edyta's Tips:

Press the seams open in your Moon Flower Petal Units, so the seams will be less bulky when you applique them to your block.

When stitching your flying geese units, start in the middle and sew out toward the edge to keep your fabric from catching in the machine.

Fabric Requirements:

Background One 20" x 21" rectangle	Fabrics A to F
Flowers Four 10" squares	Fabrics G to J
Stems and Leaves Three 10" x 15" rectangles	Fabrics K to N

Cutting:

Background
1 - 5 ½" x 21" strip, subcut into:
   3 - 5 ½" squares (A)

1 - 3 ¾" x 21" strip, subcut into:
   3 - 3 ¾" x 4" rectangles (B)

1 - 2 ⅝" x 21" strip, subcut into:
   5 - 2 ⅝" squares (C) *Cut each on the diagonal once **

1 - 2" x 21" strip, subcut into:
   3 - 2" x 3 ¾" rectangles (D)

1 - 1 ⅝" x 21" strip, subcut into:
   12 - 1 ⅝" squares (E)

1 - 1 ¼" x 21" strip, subcut into:
   1 - 1 ¼" x 12 ½" rectangle (F)

Flowers - from one fabric cut
   6 - Fabric G Flower Units (G)
   See page 53

Flowers - from one fabric cut
   3 - Fabric H Flower Units (H)
   See page 53

Flowers - from one fabric cut
   3 - Fabric I Flower Units (I)
   See page 53

Flowers - from one fabric cut
   3 - Fabric J Flower Units (J)
   See page 53

Stems and Leaves - from one fabric cut
   2 - 2 ⅝" squares (K) *Cut each on the diagonal once **
   1 - 1" x 8 ¾" rectangle (N)

Stems and Leaves - from one fabric cut
   1 - 2" x 10" rectangle (L)
   3 - 1 ⅝" x 2 ¾" rectangles (M)
   1 - 1" x 8 ¾" rectangle (N)

Stems and Leaves - from one fabric cut
   3 - 1 ⅝" x 2 ¾" rectangles (M)
   1 - 1" x 8 ¾" rectangle (N)

Moon Flower Template and Moon Flower Stem Template
   Templates are on page 108.

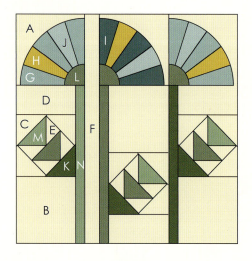

* Not all of the Fabric C triangles and Fabric K triangles will be used.

Construction:

1   Cut six Fabric G Flower Units, three Fabric H Flower Units, three Fabric I Flower Units and three Fabric J Flower Units using the Moon Flower Template.

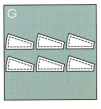

Make 6 Fabric G Flower Units.

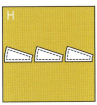

Make 3 Fabric H Flower Units.

Make 3 Fabric I Flower Units.

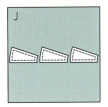

Make 3 Fabric J Flower Units.

2   Cut three Fabric L Stem Units using the Moon Flower Stem Template.

Make 3 Fabric L Stem Units.

3   Assemble three Fabric G Flower Units, one Fabric H Flower Unit and one Fabric J Flower Unit. Press open.

Make 1 Left Moon Flower Petal Unit.

4   Position the Left Moon Flower Petal Unit on the bottom right corner of a Fabric A square.

Using your applique method of choice, applique the Left Moon Flower Petal Unit in place.

Partial Left Moon Flower Unit should measure 5 ½" x 5 ½".

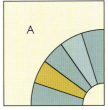

Make 1 Partial Left Moon Flower Unit.
5 ½" x 5 ½" unfinished.

5   Position a Fabric L Stem Unit on the bottom right corner of the Partial Left Moon Flower Unit.

Using your applique method of choice, applique the Fabric L Stem Unit in place.

Trim Left Moon Flower Unit to measure 4 ¼" x 4 ¼".

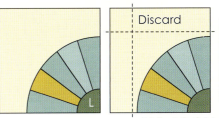

Make 1 Left Moon Flower Unit.
4 ¼" x 4 ¼" unfinished.

6   Assemble three Fabric I Flower Units, one Fabric H Flower Unit and one Fabric J Flower Unit. Press open.

Make 1 Center Moon Flower Petal Unit.

7 Position the Center Moon Flower Petal Unit on the bottom left corner of a Fabric A square.

Using your applique method of choice, applique the Center Moon Flower Petal Unit in place.

Partial Center Moon Flower Unit should measure 5 ½" x 5 ½".

Make 1 Partial Center Moon Flower Unit.
5 ½" x 5 ½" unfinished.

8 Position a Fabric L Stem Unit on the bottom left corner of the Partial Center Moon Flower Unit.

Using your applique method of choice, applique the Fabric L Stem Unit in place.

Trim Center Moon Flower Unit to measure 4 ¼" x 4 ¼".

 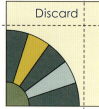

Make 1 Center Moon Flower Unit.
4 ¼" x 4 ¼" unfinished.

9 Assemble three Fabric G Flower Units, one Fabric J Flower Unit and one Fabric H Flower Unit. Press open.

Make 1 Right Moon Flower Petal Unit.

10 Position the Right Moon Flower Petal Unit on the bottom left corner of a Fabric A square.

Using your applique method of choice, applique the Right Moon Flower Petal Unit in place.

Partial Right Moon Flower Unit should measure 5 ½" x 5 ½".

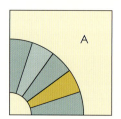

Make 1 Partial Right Moon Flower Unit.
5 ½" x 5 ½" unfinished.

11 Position a Fabric L Stem Unit on the bottom left corner of the Partial Right Moon Flower Unit.

Using your applique method of choice, applique the Fabric L Stem Unit in place.

Trim Right Moon Flower Unit to measure 4 ¼" x 4 ¼".

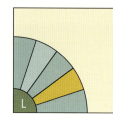 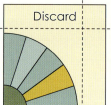

Make 1 Right Moon Flower Unit.
4 ¼" x 4 ¼" unfinished.

12 Draw a diagonal line on the wrong side of the Fabric E squares.

With right sides facing, layer a Fabric E square on one end of a Fabric M rectangle.

Stitch on the drawn line and trim ¼" away from the seam.

Repeat on the opposite end.

Make 6 Flying Geese Units.
1 ⅝" x 2 ¾" unfinished.

13 Assemble two different Flying Geese Units.

Make 3 Partial Leaf Units.
2 ¾" x 2 ¾" unfinished.

14 Assemble three Fabric C triangles, one Partial Leaf Unit and one Fabric K triangle.

Trim Leaf Unit to measure 3 ¾" x 3 ¾".

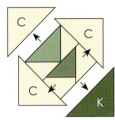

Make 3 Leaf Units.
3 ¾" x 3 ¾" unfinished.

15 Assemble one Fabric D rectangle, one Leaf Unit and one Fabric B rectangle.

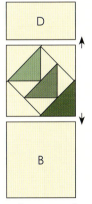

Make 1 Partial Left Moon Flower Block Unit.
3 ¾" x 8 ¾" unfinished.

16 Assemble the Left Moon Flower Unit, the Partial Left Moon Flower Block Unit and one Fabric N rectangle.

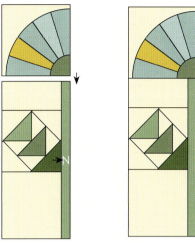

Make 1 Left Moon Flower Block Unit.
4 ¼" x 12 ½" unfinished.

17 Assemble one Fabric B rectangle, one Leaf Unit and one Fabric D rectangle.

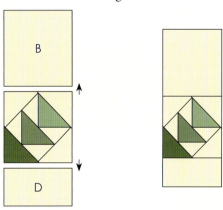

Make 1 Partial Center Moon Flower Block Unit.
3 ¾" x 8 ¾" unfinished.

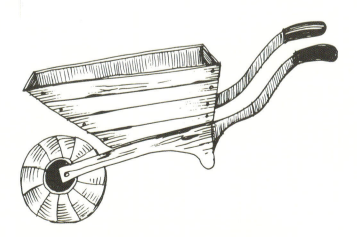

18   Assemble the Center Moon Flower Unit, one Fabric N rectangle and the Partial Center Moon Flower Block Unit.

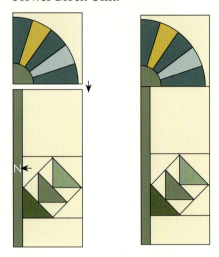

Make 1 Center Moon Flower Block Unit.
4 ¼" x 12 ½" unfinished.

19   Assemble one Fabric D rectangle, one Leaf Unit and one Fabric B rectangle.

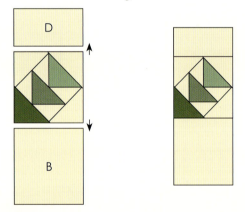

Make 1 Partial Right Moon Flower Block Unit.
3 ¾" x 8 ¾" unfinished.

20   Assemble the Right Moon Flower Unit, one Fabric N rectangle and the Partial Right Moon Flower Block Unit.

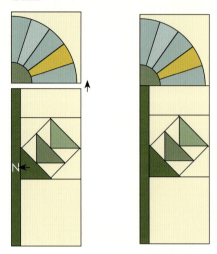

Make 1 Right Moon Flower Block Unit.
4 ¼" x 12 ½" unfinished.

21   Assemble the Left Moon Flower Block Unit, the Fabric F rectangle, the Center Moon Flower Block Unit and the Right Moon Flower Block Unit.

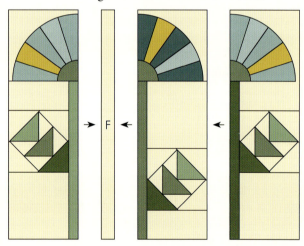

Make 1 Moon Flower Block.
12 ½" x 12 ½" unfinished.

Make 1. 12 ½" x 12 ½" unfinished.

42260-12   42265-44   42268-50   42262-38   42266-30

Fabric Requirements:

Background
½ yard

Fabrics A to N

Flowers
Two Fat Eighths (9" x 21")

Fabrics O to R

Leaves
One Fat Eighth (9" x 21")

Fabric S

Stems
One 10" x 15" rectangle

Fabrics T & U

Edyta's Tips:

When paper piecing, use an 80/12 needle and a 1.5 stitch length so the paper will easily tear away after stitching.

Cutting:

Background
2 - 3 ¾" x width of fabric strips, subcut into:

> 1 - 3 ¾" square (A) *Cut on the diagonal twice* *
> 1 - 3" x 4 ½" rectangle (B)
> 5 - 2 ½" x 4 ½" rectangles (C)
> 5 - 2 ½" x 4 ½" rectangles (D)

1 - 2 ¼" x width of fabric strip, subcut into:

> 5 - 2 ¼" x 3 ½" rectangles (E)
> 1 - 2 ¼" x 3" rectangle (F)
> 3 - 2 ¼" squares (G)
> 3 - 2 ⅛" squares (H) *Cut each on the diagonal once*

1 - 2" x width of fabric strip, subcut into:

> 1 - 2" x 3 ¼" rectangle (I)
> 3 - 2" x 3" rectangles (J)
> 10 - 1 ⅞" squares (K)

1 - 1 ¾" x width of fabric strip, subcut into:

> 2 - 1 ¾" x 3 ¼" rectangles (L)
> 1 - 1 ½" x 3 ¼" rectangle (M)
> 1 - 1" x 3 ¼" rectangle (N)

Flowers - from one fabric cut

> 3 - 2 ¼" squares (O)
> 5 - 1 ⅞" x 3 ¼" rectangles (P)

Flowers - from one fabric cut

> 1 - 3 ¾" square (Q) *Cut on the diagonal twice* *
> 3 - 2 ⅛" squares (R) *Cut each on the diagonal once*

Leaves

> 5 - 4" squares (S)

Stems

> 2 - ⅞" x 10" rectangles (T)
> 1 - ¾" x 7 ½" rectangle (U)

Sweet Pea Leaf Paper Piecing Template

> Template is on page 109.

* *Not all of the Fabric A triangles and Fabric Q triangles will be used.*

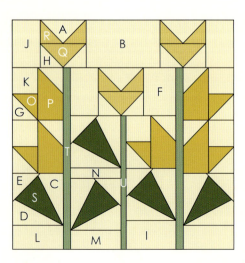

Construction:

1 Draw a diagonal line on the wrong side of the Fabric G squares.

With right sides facing, layer a Fabric G square with a Fabric O square.

Stitch ¼" from each side of the drawn line. Cut apart on the marked line.

One of the Half Square Triangle Units will not be used.

Make 6 Half Square Triangle Units.
1 ⅞" x 1 ⅞" unfinished.

2 Draw a diagonal line on the wrong side of five Fabric K squares.

With right sides facing, layer a marked Fabric K square on the top end of a Fabric P rectangle.

Stitch on the drawn line and trim ¼" away from the seam.

Make 3 Partial Left Flower Units.
1 ⅞" x 3 ¼" unfinished.

3 Assemble one unmarked Fabric K square, one Half Square Triangle Unit and one Partial Left Flower Unit.

Make 3 Left Flower Units.
3 ¼" x 3 ¼" unfinished.

4 With right sides facing, layer a marked Fabric K square on the top end of a Fabric P rectangle.

Stitch on the drawn line and trim ¼" away from the seam.

Make 2 Partial Right Flower Units.
1 ⅞" x 3 ¼" unfinished.

5 Assemble one Partial Right Flower Unit, one Fabric K square and one Half Square Triangle Unit.

Make 2 Right Flower Units.
3 ¼" x 3 ¼" unfinished.

6 Assemble two Fabric R triangles and one Fabric A triangle.

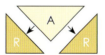

Make 3 Top Flying Geese Units.
1 ¾" x 3" unfinished.

7 Assemble two Fabric H triangles and one Fabric Q triangle.

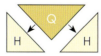

Make 3 Bottom Flying Geese Units.
1 ¾" x 3" unfinished.

8 Assemble one Top Flying Geese Unit and one Bottom Flying Geese Unit.

Make 3 Top Flower Units.
3" x 3" unfinished.

9   Layer the Sweet Pea Leaf Paper Piecing Template right side facing down and a Fabric S square right side facing up, so the Fabric S square completely covers the template.

Make 5.

10   Place one Fabric D rectangle right side down on the Fabric S square so the area will be completely covered once sewn. Make sure there is a ¼" seam on all sides. Pin in place.

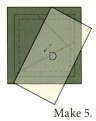

Make 5.

11   Use a shorter stitch length, around 1.5, so the paper will tear easier.

Turn over the unit so the template is on top and stitch on the appropriate solid line.

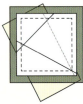

Make 5.

12   Fold the template at the stitch line and trim unit ¼" from the stitch line. Do not trim the template. Turn unit over and press flat.

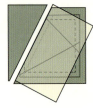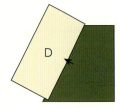

Make 5.

13   Repeat to complete the Partial Sweet Pea Leaf Unit. Press flat.

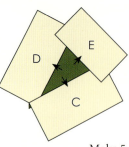

Make 5.

14   Trim the Sweet Pea Leaf Unit to measure 3 ¼" x 3 ¼".

Tear template paper away.

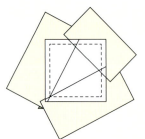

Make 5 Sweet Pea Leaf Units.
3 ¼" x 3 ¼" unfinished.

15   Assemble two Left Flower Units, one Sweet Pea Leaf Unit and one Fabric L rectangle.

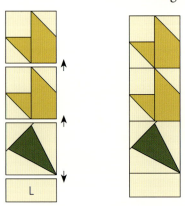

Make 1 Left Sweet Pea Unit.
3 ¼" x 10" unfinished.

16 Assemble three Sweet Pea Leaf Units, the Fabric N rectangle, the Fabric M rectangle, one Left Flower Unit, the Fabric I rectangle and the Fabric U rectangle.

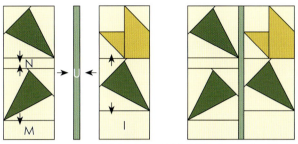

Make 1 Partial Middle Sweet Pea Unit.
6 ¼" x 7 ½" unfinished.

17 Assemble one Fabric J rectangle, one Top Flower Unit, the Fabric F rectangle and the Partial Middle Sweet Pea Unit.

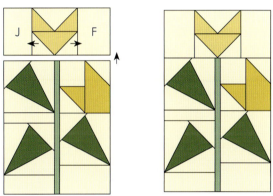

Make 1 Middle Sweet Pea Unit.
6 ¼" x 10" unfinished.

18 Assemble two Right Flower Units, one Sweet Pea Leaf Unit and one Fabric L rectangle.

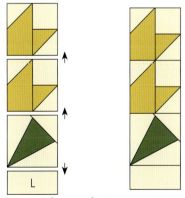

Make 1 Right Sweet Pea Unit.
3 ¼" x 10" unfinished.

19 Assemble two Fabric J rectangles, two Top Flower Units and the Fabric B rectangle.

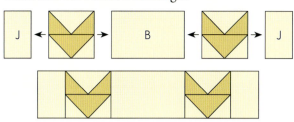

Make 1 Top Sweet Pea Unit.
3" x 12 ½" unfinished.

20 Assemble the Top Sweet Pea Unit, the Left Sweet Pea Unit, two Fabric T rectangles, the Middle Sweet Pea Unit and the Right Sweet Pea Unit.

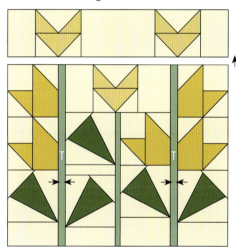

Make 1 Sweet Pea Block.
12 ½" x 12 ½" unfinished.

Make 1. 12 ½" x 12 ½" unfinished.

42266-12 42264-34 42261-42 42266-30 42261-38

Fabric Requirements:

Background One Fat Quarter (18" x 21")	Fabrics A to I
Flowers Two 10" squares	Fabric J
Leaves One 10" square	Fabric K
Stems and Leaves One Fat Eighth (9" x 21")	Fabrics K, L & M

Edyta's Tips:

When using Triangle paper to make Half Square Triangles, use an 80/12 needle and a 1.5 stitch length so the paper will easily tear away after stitching.

Using plenty of pins when piecing Eight Point Stars will help you have a perfect ¼" seam allowance.

Cutting:

Background

1 - 6" x 21" strip, subcut into:
    2 - 6" squares (A)
    1 - 2 ½" x 4 ½" rectangle (B)

1 - 2 ¼" x 21" strip, subcut into:
    2 - 2 ¼" x 3 ¼" rectangles (C)
    1 - 2 ¼" x 3" rectangle (D)
    3 - 2 ¼" squares (E)
    2 - 1 ½" x 2 ¼" rectangles (F)
    1 - 1 ¼" x 2 ¼" rectangle (G)

1 - 2 ⅞" x 21" strip, subcut into:
    3 - 2 ⅞" squares (H) *Cut each on the diagonal twice*

1 - 1 ⅝" x 21" strip, subcut into:
    12 - 1 ⅝" squares (I)

Flowers - from each fabric cut
    3 - 1 ⅜" x 10" rectangles (J)

Leaves
    1 - 6" square (K)

Stems and Leaves
    1 - 6" square (K)
    2 - 1" x 8 ½" rectangles (L)
    1 - 1" x 6 ½" rectangle (M)

1 ¾" Half Square Triangle Paper
    Half Square Triangle Paper is on page 109.

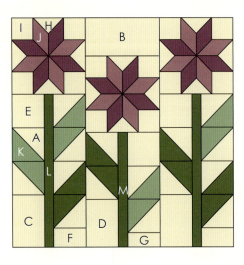

Construction:

1 With right sides facing, layer a Fabric K square with a Fabric A square.

Place the 1 ¾" Half Square Triangle Paper on top and pin in place.

Set stitch length to 1.5 and sew on the dotted lines.

Cut apart on the solid lines.

Make 16 Half Square Triangle Units.
2 ¼" x 2 ¼" unfinished.

2 Layer two different Fabric J rectangles right sides together.

Align the 45° line on the ruler and trim the left edge of the Fabric J rectangle.

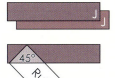 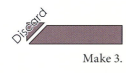

Make 3.

3 Cut four 1 ⅜" wide diamonds from each strip set.

Keep diamonds right sides together.

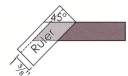 

Make 12 Diamond Units.

4 With the tip of the Diamond Unit at the top right, begin your stitch ¼" away from the top edge and end ¼" away from the bottom edge of the Diamond Unit. Backstitch.

Make 12 Quarter Star Point Units.

5 With right sides facing, layer two Quarter Star Point Units. Begin stitching at the top right edge and end ¼" away from the bottom edge. Backstitch.

Make 6 Half Star Point Units.

6 With right sides facing, layer two Half Star Point Units. Begin stitching slightly before the center to ¼" away from the edge. Backstitch.

Repeat on the opposite end, overlapping stitches.

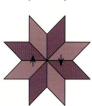

Make 3 Star Point Units.

7 Fold the Star Point Unit in half. With right sides facing, attach one Fabric H triangle to one Star Point Unit. Begin at the outside edge of the Fabric H triangle and end ¼" away from the edge. Backstitch.

Refold the Star Point Unit in half so the other edge of the Fabric H triangle matches up with a new point. Begin at the outside edge of the Fabric H triangle and end ¼" away from the edge. Backstitch.

 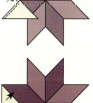

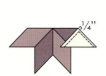

Make 3 Partial Star Flower Units.

8   Repeat on the remaining three sides of the Partial Star Flower Unit.

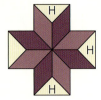

Make 3 Partial Star Flower Units.

9   Fold the Partial Star Point Unit in half. With right sides facing, attach one Fabric I square to one Partial Star Flower Unit. Begin at the outside edge of the Fabric I square and end ¼" away from the edge. Backstitch.

Refold the Partial Star Flower Unit in half so the other edge of the Fabric I square matches up with a new point. Begin at the outside edge of the Fabric I square and end ¼" away from the edge. Backstitch.

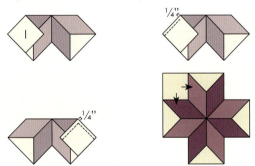

Make 3 Partial Star Flower Units.

10   Repeat on the remaining three corners of the Partial Star Flower Unit.

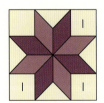

Make 3 Star Flower Units.
4 ½" x 4 ½" unfinished.

11   Assemble one Fabric E square, four matching Half Square Triangle Units, one Fabric C rectangle, one Fabric L rectangle, two matching Half Square Triangle Units and one Fabric F rectangle.

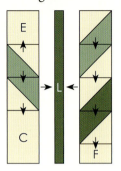

Make 1 Left Stem Unit.
4 ½" x 8 ½" unfinished.

12   Assemble one Star Flower Unit and the Left Stem Unit.

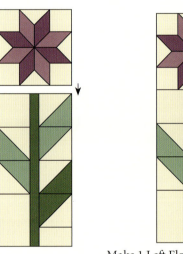

Make 1 Left Flower Unit.
4 ½" x 12 ½" unfinished.

13   Assemble two matching Half Square Triangle Units, the Fabric D rectangle, the Fabric M rectangle, one Fabric E square, two matching Half Square Triangle Units and the Fabric G rectangle.

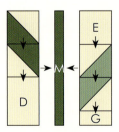

Make 1 Center Stem Unit.
4 ½" x 6 ½" unfinished.

14 Assemble the Fabric B rectangle, one Star Flower Unit and the Center Stem Unit.

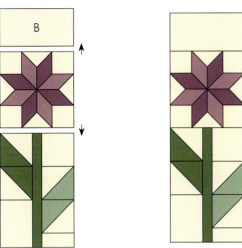

Make 1 Center Flower Unit.
4 ½" x 12 ½" unfinished.

15 Assemble one Fabric E square, four matching Half Square Triangle Units, one Fabric C rectangle, one Fabric L rectangle, two matching Half Square Triangle Units and one Fabric F rectangle.

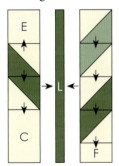

Make 1 Right Stem Unit.
4 ½" x 8 ½" unfinished.

16 Assemble one Star Flower Unit and the Right Stem Unit.

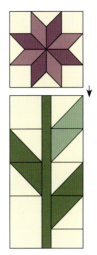

Make 1 Right Flower Unit.
4 ½" x 12 ½" unfinished.

17 Assemble the Left Flower Unit, the Center Flower Unit and the Right Flower Unit.

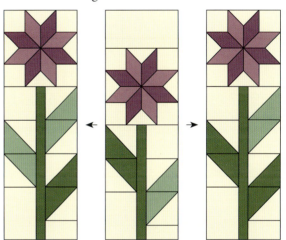

Make 1 Bachelor Button Block.
12 ½" x 12 ½" unfinished.

Make 1. 12 ½" x 24 ½" unfinished.

42268-12   42264-41   42265-40   42268-46   42265-27

42266-30   42261-38

Edyta's Tips:

Freezer paper works beautifully as template paper and helps you cut wonderful curves with ease.

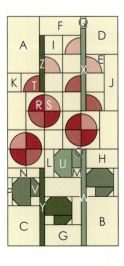

Fabric Requirements:

Background ⅔ yard	Fabrics A to Q
Flowers Three 10" squares	Fabrics R, S & T
Leaves One 10" square	Fabrics U & V
Stems and Leaves Two 10" x 15" rectangles	Fabrics U to Z

Cutting:

Background

1 - 4" x width of fabric strip, subcut into:
- 1 - 4" x 6 ½" rectangle (A)
- 1 - 4" x 5 ½" rectangle (B)
- 1 - 4" x 4 ¾" rectangle (C)
- 1 - 4" x 4 ½" rectangle (D)

2 - 3 ½" x width of fabric strips, subcut into:
- 18 - 3 ½" squares (E)

2 - 2 ½" x width of fabric strips, subcut into:
- 1 - 2 ½" x 5" rectangle (F)
- 4 - 2 ½" x 4 ½" rectangles (G)
- 1 - 2 ½" x 4" rectangle (H)
- 6 - 2 ½" squares (I)

1 - 2" x width of fabric strip, subcut into:
- 1 - 2" x 6 ½" rectangle (J)
- 1 - 2" x 2 ½" rectangle (K)
- 2 - 1 ½" x 3 ½" rectangles (L)
- 4 - 1 ½" squares (M)

1 - 1 ¼" x width of fabric strip, subcut into:
- 1 - 1 ¼" x 4" rectangle (N)
- 12 - 1 ¼" squares (O)
- 2 - 1" x 3 ½" rectangles (P)
- 1 - 1" x 1 ¾" rectangle (Q)

Flowers - from one fabric cut
- 6 - Fabric R Units (R)
- *See page 67*

Flowers - from one fabric cut
- 6 - Fabric S Units (S)
- *See page 67*

Flowers - from one fabric cut
- 6 - Fabric T Units (T)
- *See page 67*

Leaves
- 2 - 2 ½" x 3 ½" rectangles (U)
- 2 - 1 ½" x 2 ½" rectangles (V)

Stems and Leaves - from one fabric cut
- 1 - 2 ½" x 3 ½" rectangle (U)
- 1 - 1 ½" x 2 ½" rectangle (V)
- 1 - 1" x 10 ½" rectangle (W)
- 1 - 1" x 9 ¼" rectangle (X)

Stems and Leaves - from one fabric cut
- 1 - 2 ½" x 3 ½" rectangle (U)
- 1 - 1 ½" x 2 ½" rectangle (V)
- 1 - 1" x 8 ½" rectangle (Y)
- 1 - 1" x 6 ½" rectangle (Z)

Hollyhock Flower Template
Template is on page 109.

Construction:

1 Using the Hollyhock Flower Template, cut six Fabric R Units, six Fabric S Units and six Fabric T Units.

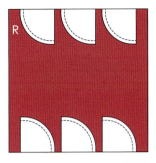

Make 6 Fabric R Units.

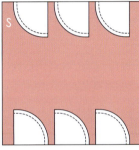

Make 6 Fabric S Units.

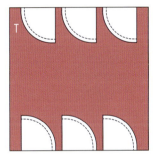

Make 6 Fabric T Units.

2 Position a Fabric R Unit on the bottom left corner of a Fabric E square. Using your applique method of choice, applique the Fabric R Unit in place.

Repeat for the Fabric S Units and Fabric T Units.

Trim Units to measure 2 ½" x 2 ½".

Make 6 Fabric R Quarter Flower Units.
2 ½" x 2 ½" unfinished.

Make 6 Fabric S Quarter Flower Units.
2 ½" x 2 ½" unfinished.

Make 6 Fabric T Quarter Flower Units.
2 ½" x 2 ½" unfinished.

3 Draw a diagonal line on the wrong side of the Fabric O squares.

With right sides facing, layer a Fabric O square on the top left corner of a Fabric U rectangle.

Stitch on the drawn line and trim ¼" away from the seam.

Repeat on the bottom left corner.

Make 4 Large Leaf Units.
2 ½" x 3 ½" unfinished.

4 With right sides facing, layer a Fabric O square on the top right corner of a Fabric V rectangle.

Stitch on the drawn line and trim ¼" away from the seam.

Make 4 Partial Small Leaf Units.
1 ½" x 2 ½" unfinished.

5 Assemble one Partial Small Leaf Unit, one Fabric M square and one matching Large Leaf Unit.

Make 4 Leaf Units.
3 ½" x 3 ½" unfinished.

6 Assemble the Fabric N rectangle, one Fabric P rectangle, one Leaf Unit and the Fabric C rectangle.

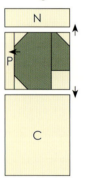 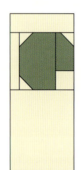

Make 1 Bottom Left Leaf Unit.
4" x 8 ½" unfinished.

7 Assemble the Bottom Left Leaf Unit and the Fabric Y rectangle.

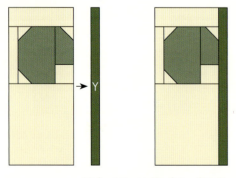

Make 1 Partial Left Leaf Unit.
4 ½" x 8 ½" unfinished.

8 Assemble one Fabric R Quarter Flower Unit, one Fabric T Quarter Flower Unit and the Partial Left Leaf Unit.

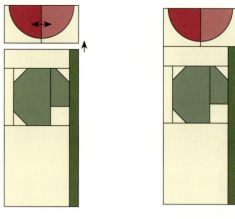

Make 1 Left Leaf Unit.
4 ½" x 10 ½" unfinished.

9 Assemble two Fabric L rectangles, two different Leaf Units and two Fabric G rectangles.

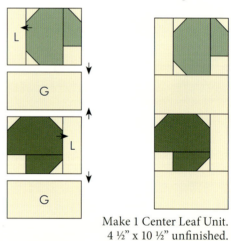

Make 1 Center Leaf Unit.
4 ½" x 10 ½" unfinished.

10 Assemble the Fabric H rectangle, one Leaf Unit, one Fabric P rectangle and the Fabric B rectangle.

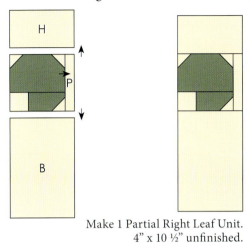

Make 1 Partial Right Leaf Unit.
4" x 10 ½" unfinished.

11 Assemble the Fabric W rectangle and the Partial Right Leaf Unit.

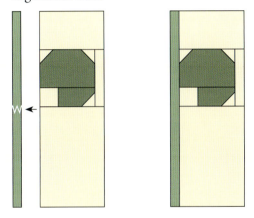

Make 1 Right Leaf Unit.
4 ½" x 10 ½" unfinished.

12 Assemble the Left Leaf Unit, the Center Leaf Unit and the Right Leaf Unit.

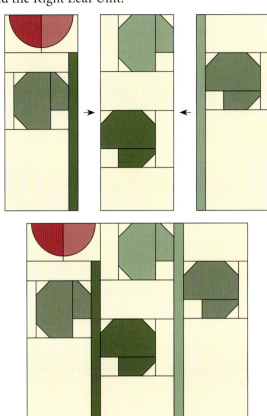

Make 1 Bottom Hollyhock Unit.
10 ½" x 12 ½" unfinished.

13 Assemble three Fabric R Quarter Flower Units, one Fabric S Quarter Flower Unit, one Fabric T Quarter Flower Unit and one Fabric I square.

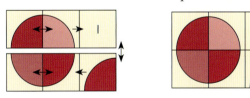

Make 1 Partial Middle Hollyhock Unit.
4 ½" x 6 ½" unfinished.

14 Assemble one Fabric G rectangle, the Partial Middle Hollyhock Unit, one Fabric S Quarter Flower Unit, one Fabric R Quarter Flower Unit, one Fabric I square and one Fabric T Quarter Flower Unit.

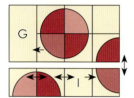
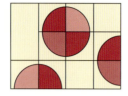

Make 1 Middle Hollyhock Unit.
6 ½" x 8 ½" unfinished.

15 Assemble the Fabric A rectangle, the Fabric K rectangle and one Fabric T Quarter Flower Unit.

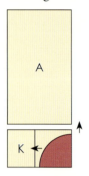

Make 1 Top Left Hollyhock Unit.
4" x 8 ½" unfinished.

16 Assemble three Fabric I squares, two Fabric S Quarter Flower Units and one Fabric T Quarter Flower Unit.

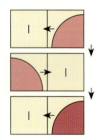
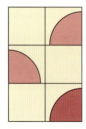

Make 1 Partial Top Middle Hollyhock Unit.
4 ½" x 6 ½" unfinished.

17 Assemble the Fabric F rectangle, the Fabric Z rectangle and the Partial Top Middle Hollyhock Unit.

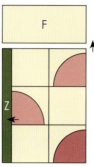
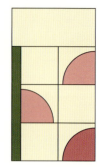

Make 1 Top Middle Hollyhock Unit.
5" x 8 ½" unfinished.

18 Assemble one Fabric S Quarter Flower Unit, one Fabric I square, one Fabric T Quarter Flower Unit and the Fabric J rectangle.

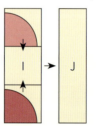
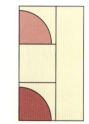

Make 1 Incomplete Partial Top Right Hollyhock Unit.
4" x 6 ½" unfinished.

19 Assemble the Fabric Q rectangle, the Fabric X rectangle, the Fabric D rectangle and the Incomplete Partial Top Right Hollyhock Unit.

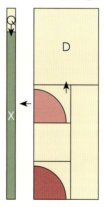
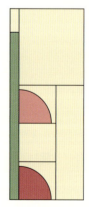

Make 1 Partial Top Right Hollyhock Unit.
4 ½" x 10 ½" unfinished.

20 Assemble the Partial Top Right Hollyhock Unit, one Fabric S Quarter Flower Unit, one Fabric R Quarter Flower Unit and one Fabric G rectangle.

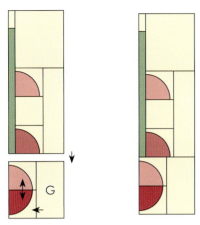

Make 1 Top Right Hollyhock Unit.
4 ½" x 14 ½" unfinished.

21 Assemble the Top Left Hollyhock Unit, the Top Middle Hollyhock Unit and the Middle Hollyhock Unit.

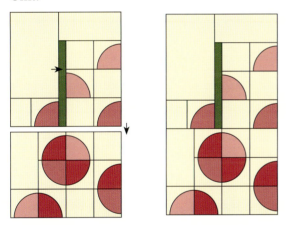

Make 1 Partial Top Hollyhock Unit.
8 ½" x 14 ½" unfinished.

22 Assemble the Partial Top Hollyhock Unit and the Top Right Hollyhock Unit.

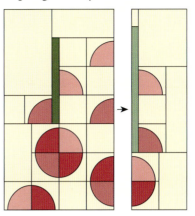

Make 1 Top Hollyhock Unit.
12 ½" x 14 ½" unfinished.

23 Assemble the Top Hollyhock Unit and the Bottom Hollyhock Unit.

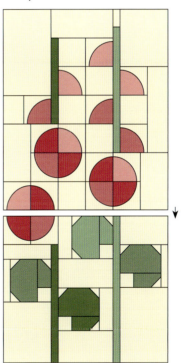

Make 1 Hollyhock Block.
12 ½" x 24 ½" unfinished.

Make 1. 12 ½" x 24 ½" unfinished.

42260-12   42261-32   42260-31   42264-39   42260-22

42261-37   42262-24   42268-44   42265-34

Edyta's Tips:

I used interfacing as a stabilizer to turn under the edges on the clamshell roof shingles. Interfacing makes the curves perfectly smooth.

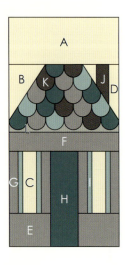

Fabric Requirements:

Background One Fat Quarter (18" x 21")	Fabrics A to D
House One Fat Quarter (18" x 21")	Fabrics E, F & G
Door One 10" x 15" rectangle	Fabric H
Shutters One 10" square	Fabric I
Chimney and Roof Shingles One Fat Eighth (9" x 21")	Fabrics J & K
Roof Shingles Three Fat Eighths (9" x 21")	Fabric K
Roof Base One 10" x 15" rectangle	Fabric L
Stabilizer One Fat Eighth (9" x 21")	Fabric M

Cutting:

Background
1 - 5 ½" x 21" strip, subcut into:
    1 - 5 ½" x 12 ½" rectangle (A)
    1 - 4 ¾" x 6 ½" rectangle (B)

1 - 2" x 21" strip, subcut into:
    2 - 2" x 7" rectangles (C)

1 - 1 ¾" x 21" strip, subcut into:
    2 - 1 ¾" x 6 ⅜" rectangles (D)

House
1 - 4" x 21" strip, subcut into:
    2 - 4" x 5" rectangles (E)

1 - 2 ½" x 21" strip, subcut into:
    1 - 2 ½" x 12 ½" rectangle (F)

2 - 1 ½" x 21" strips, subcut into:
    4 - 1 ½" x 7" rectangles (G)

Door
1 - 3 ½" x 10 ½" rectangle (H)

Shutters
    4 - 1" x 7" rectangles (I)

Chimney and Roof Shingles
    1 - 2" x 6 ⅜" rectangle (J)
    1 - 4 ¼" x 21" strip (K)

Roof Shingles - from each fabric cut
    1 - 4 ¼" x 21" strip (K)

Roof Base
    1 - 4" x 12 ½" rectangle (L)

Stabilizer
    4 - 1 ¾" x 21" strips (M)

Clamshell Template, Stabilizer Template, Background Roof Templates and Roof Templates
    Templates are on pages 110 to 112.

Construction:

1 Assemble two Fabric G rectangles, two Fabric I rectangles and one Fabric C rectangle.

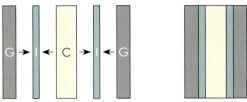

Make 2 Window Units.
5" x 7" unfinished.

2 Assemble one Window Unit and one Fabric E rectangle.

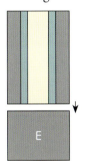
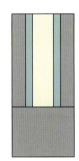

Make 2 Partial House Units.
5" x 10 ½" unfinished.

3 Assemble two Partial House Units, the Fabric H rectangle and the Fabric F rectangle.

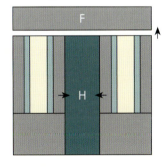
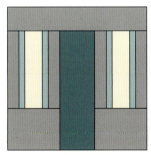

Make 1 House Unit.
12 ½" x 12 ½" unfinished.

4 Cut 20 Partial Clamshell Units using the Clamshell Template and 20 Stabilizer Units using the Stabilizer Template.

Draw an arch line on the Partial Clamshell Units and the Stabilizer Units according to the templates.

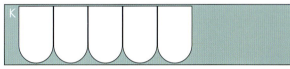

Make 20 Partial Clamshell Units.

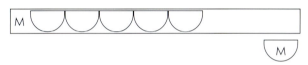

Make 20 Stabilizer Units.

5 With right sides facing, layer a Partial Clamshell Unit with a Stabilizer Unit.

Stitch on the drawn arch line. Backstitch at the beginning and end.

Trim the unit ⅛" away from the stitch line.

Turn the Clamshell Unit right side out. Press.

Make 20 Clamshell Units.

6 Align the top edges of six Clamshell Units

Stitch with a ¼" seam along the side, making sure to backstitch at the beginning and end.

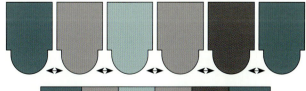

Make 1 First Roof Row Unit.

7   Align the top edges of five Clamshell Units.

Stitch with a ¼" seam along the side, making sure to backstitch at the beginning and end.

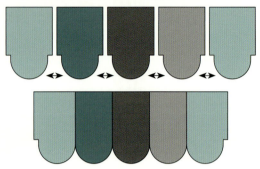

Make 1 Second Roof Row Unit.

8   Align the top edges of four Clamshell Units.

Stitch with a ¼" seam along the side, making sure to backstitch at the beginning and end.

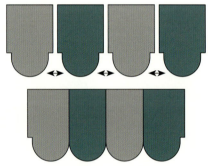

Make 1 Third Roof Row Unit.

9   Align the top edges of three Clamshell Units.

Stitch with a ¼" seam along the side, making sure to backstitch at the beginning and end.

Make 1 Fourth Roof Row Unit.

10   Align the top edges of two Clamshell Units.

Stitch with a ¼" seam along the side, making sure to backstitch at the beginning and end.

Make 1 Fifth Roof Row Unit.

11   Stay stitch or zig zag stitch the top edge of the Fabric L rectangle to avoid fraying during the piecing process.

Mark the center of the Fabric L rectangle.

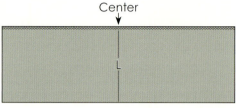

Make 1.

12   Fold the First Roof Row Unit in half. Finger press the center.

Align the center of the row with the center of the Fabric L rectangle.

Draw a line 2 ¾" up from the bottom edge of the First Roof Row Unit. Use a basting stitch on the drawn line.

Using your applique method of choice, applique the row of curved ends to the Fabric L rectangle.

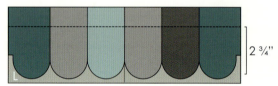

Make 1 Partial Roof Unit.

13   Measure 1 ⅜" up from the bottom edge of the First Roof Row Unit. Use this guideline to arrange the Second Roof Row Unit.

Fold the Second Roof Row Unit in half. Finger press the center.

Align the center of the row with the center of the Partial Roof Unit.

Using your applique method of choice, applique the row of curved ends to the Partial Roof Unit.

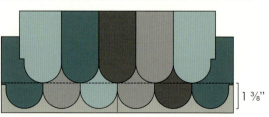

Make 1 Partial Roof Unit.

14 Measure 1 ⅜" up from the bottom edge of the Second Roof Row Unit. Use this guideline to arrange the Third Roof Row Unit.

Fold the Third Roof Row Unit in half. Finger press the center.

Align the center of the row with the center of the Partial Roof Unit.

Using your applique method of choice, applique the row of curved ends to the Partial Roof Unit.

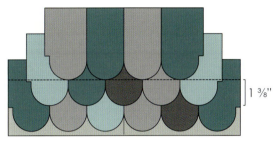

1 ⅜"

Make 1 Partial Roof Unit.

15 Measure 1 ⅜" up from the bottom edge of the Third Roof Row Unit. Use this guideline to arrange the Fourth Roof Row Unit.

Fold the Fourth Roof Row Unit in half. Finger press the center.

Align the center of the row with the center of the Partial Roof Unit.

Using your applique method of choice, applique the row of curved ends to the Partial Roof Unit.

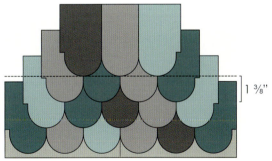

1 ⅜"

Make 1 Partial Roof Unit.

16 Measure 1 ⅜" up from the bottom edge of the Fourth Roof Row Unit. Use this guideline to arrange the Fifth Roof Row Unit.

Fold the Fifth Roof Row Unit in half. Finger press the center.

Align the center of the row with the center of the Partial Roof Unit.

Using your applique method of choice, applique the row of curved ends to the Partial Roof Unit.

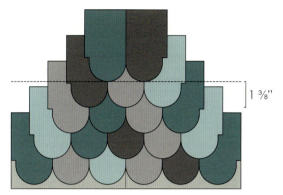

1 ⅜"

Make 1 Partial Roof Unit.

17 Tape the Left Half Roof Template and the Right Half Roof Template together to create the Complete Roof Template.

Align the Complete Roof Template on the bottom edge of the Partial Roof Unit and trim around the template.

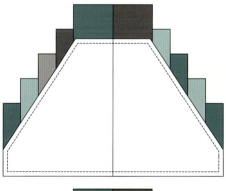

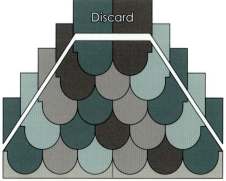

Discard

Make 1 Partial Roof Unit.

18 Assemble two Fabric D rectangles and the Fabric J rectangle.

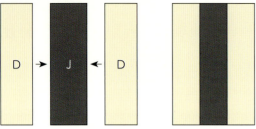

Make 1 Partial Chimney Unit.
4 ½" x 6 ⅜" unfinished.

19 Align the Right Background Roof Template on the top right edge of the Partial Chimney Unit and trim around the template.

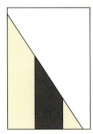

Make 1 Chimney Unit.

20 Align the Left Background Roof Template on the top left edge of the Fabric B rectangle, trim around the template.

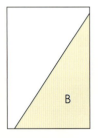

Make 1 Left Roof Unit.

21 Assemble the Left Roof Unit, the Partial Roof Unit and the Chimney Unit.

Trim Complete Roof Unit to measure 7 ½" x 12 ½".

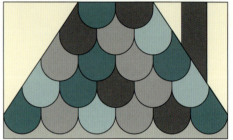

Make 1 Complete Roof Unit.
7 ½" x 12 ½" unfinished.

22 Assemble the Fabric A rectangle, the Complete Roof Unit and the House Unit.

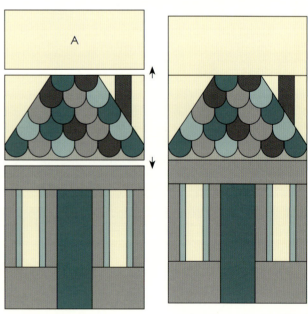

Make 1 Greenhouse Block.
12 ½" x 24 ½" unfinished.

SUNFLOWER BLOCK

Make 1. 12 ½" x 24 ½" unfinished.

42268-12   42268-50   42265-44   42261-32   42262-38

42266-30   42261-38

Edyta's Tips:

Use a 1.5 stitch length when stitching closed the tops of the Dresden Units to help your points hold together when turning.

Be careful not to trim too much of the seam allowance when trimming the Dresden Units before turning.

Fabric Requirements:

Background ½ yard	Fabrics A to N
Flowers Two 10" x 15" rectangles	Fabric O
Flower Accent One 10" square	Fabric P
Leaves Two 10" squares	Fabrics Q & R
Stems and Leaves One Fat Eighth (9" x 21")	Fabrics Q, R & S

Cutting:

Background
1 - 6 ¾" x width of fabric strip, subcut into:
- 1 - 6 ¾" x 12 ½" rectangle (A)
- 1 - 5" square (B)
- 1 - 3 ¾" x 6" rectangle (C)
- 1 - 3 ¾" x 5" rectangle (D)
- 1 - 3 ¾" x 4 ¾" rectangle (E)
- 1 - 3" x 3 ¾" rectangle (F)

1 - 2 ½" x width of fabric strip, subcut into:
- 1 - 2 ½" x 5" rectangle (G)
- 2 - 2 ½" x 3" rectangles (H)
- 1 - 2 ¼" x 3 ¾" rectangle (I)
- 2 - 2" x 5" rectangles (J)
- 2 - 2" x 3 ¾" rectangles (K)
- 1 - 1 ¾" x 3 ¾" rectangle (L)

1 - 1 ¾" x width of fabric strip, subcut into:
- 16 - 1 ¾" squares (M)
- 3 - 1 ¼" x 3" rectangles (N)

Flowers - from each fabric cut
- 2 - 2 ¾" x 12" rectangles (O)

Flower Accent
- 2 - Sunflower Center Units (P)
- *See page 79*

Leaves - from one fabric cut
- 1 - 3 ¾" square (Q)
- 2 - 3" squares (R)

Leaves - from one fabric cut
- 1 - 3 ¾" square (Q)
- 1 - 3" square (R)

Stems and Leaves
- 1 - 3 ¾" square (Q)
- 2 - 3" squares (R)
- 2 - 1" x 18 ¼" rectangles (S)

Sunflower Dresden Template and Sunflower Center Template
Templates are on page 113.

Construction:

1   Using the Sunflower Dresden Template, cut thirty-two Fabric O Units.

Make 16 Fabric O1 Units.

Make 16 Fabric O2 Units.

2   Using the Sunflower Center Template, cut two Fabric P Units.

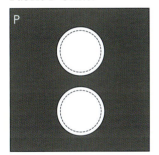

Make 2 Sunflower Center Units.

3   With right sides together, fold each Fabric O Unit lengthwise matching the wide top end. Stitch top closed. Backstitch to secure seam.

Trim the corner at the top end of the Fabric O Unit.

Turn the Fabric O Unit right side out. Press flat.

Make 16 Dresden O1 Units.

Make 16 Dresden O2 Units.

4   Assemble eight Dresden O1 Units and eight Dresden O2 Units.

Start stitching at outside edge and backstitch to secure seam. Press open.

Make 2 Partial Sunflower Units.

5   Position one Sunflower Center Unit in the center of one Partial Sunflower Unit.

Using your applique method of choice, applique the Sunflower Center Unit in place.

Make 2 Sunflower Units.

6   Draw a diagonal line on the wrong side of the Fabric M squares.

With right sides facing, layer a Fabric M square on the top right corner of a Fabric R square.

Stitch on the drawn line and trim ¼" away from the seam.

Repeat on the bottom left corner.

Make 5 Small Leaf Units.
3" x 3" unfinished.

7 With right sides facing, layer a Fabric M square on the top left corner of a Fabric Q square.

Stitch on the drawn line and trim ¼" away from the seam.

Repeat on the bottom right corner.

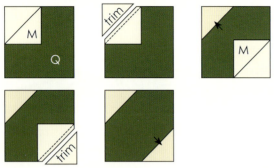

Make 3 Large Leaf Units.
3 ¾" x 3 ¾" unfinished.

8 Assemble three Fabric N rectangles, three Small Leaf Units, the Fabric F rectangle, one Fabric K rectangle, the Fabric I rectangle and the Fabric D rectangle.

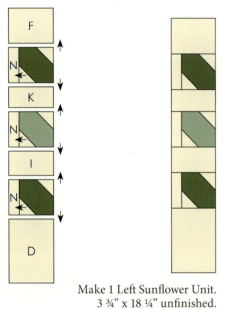

Make 1 Left Sunflower Unit.
3 ¾" x 18 ¼" unfinished.

9 Assemble two Small Leaf Units, two Fabric H rectangles, one Large Leaf Unit, the Fabric L rectangle, the Fabric B square, two Fabric J rectangles and the Fabric G rectangle.

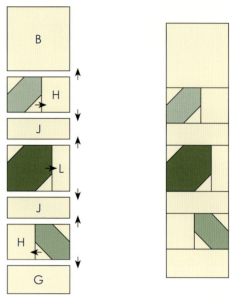

Make 1 Center Sunflower Unit.
5" x 18 ¼" unfinished.

10 Assemble the Fabric E rectangle, two Large Leaf Units, one Fabric K rectangle and the Fabric C rectangle.

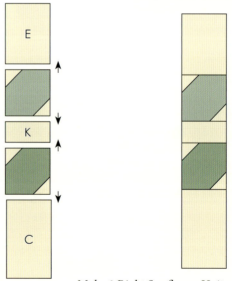

Make 1 Right Sunflower Unit.
3 ¾" x 18 ¼" unfinished.

11 Assemble the Left Sunflower Unit, two Fabric S rectangles, the Center Sunflower Unit, the Right Sunflower Unit and the Fabric A rectangle.

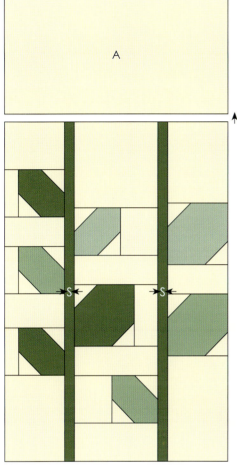

Make 1 Partial Sunflower Block Unit.
12 ½" x 24 ½" unfinished.

12 Position the two Sunflower Units on the Partial Sunflower Block Unit.

Using your applique method of choice, applique the Sunflower Units in place.

Make 1 Sunflower Block.
12 ½" x 24 ½" unfinished.

Make 3. 8 ½" x 8 ½" unfinished.

42260-12   42264-39   42260-31   42261-42   42260-22

Fabric Requirements:

Background
One Fat Quarter (18" x 21")   Fabrics A, B & C

Butterfly Wings
Three 10" squares   Fabric D

Butterfly Bodies
One 10" square   Fabric E

Cutting:

Background

2 - 4 ½" x 21" strips (A)

1 - 3 ¼" x 21" strip, subcut into:
   6 - 3 ¼" squares (B) *Cut each on the diagonal once*

1 - 1 ¼" x 21" strip, subcut into:
   6 - 1 ¼" squares (C)

Butterfly Wings - from each fabric cut
   2 - 4 ½" x 10" rectangles (D)

Butterfly Bodies
   3 - 1 ¼" x 7" rectangles (E)

Butterfly Wing Template and Antennae Embroidery Template
   Templates are on page 113.

Charcoal Embroidery Floss

Edyta's Tips:

Don't forget to add the finishing touch to your butterfly with three strands of embroidery floss for the butterfly's antennae.

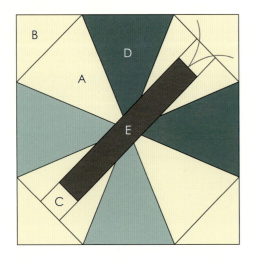

Construction:

1 Assemble two Fabric C squares and one Fabric E rectangle.

Make 3 Butterfly Body Units.
1 ¼" x 8 ½" unfinished.

2 Using the Butterfly Wing Template, cut six Fabric A triangles from each Fabric A strip, and two Fabric D triangles from each Fabric D rectangle.

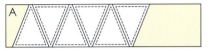

Make 12 Fabric A Triangle Units.

Make 12 Fabric D Triangle Units.

3 Assemble two Fabric A Triangle Units and two matching Fabric D Triangle Units.

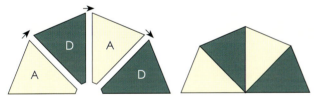

Make 6 Half Butterfly Wings Units.

4 Assemble two different Half Butterfly Wings Units.

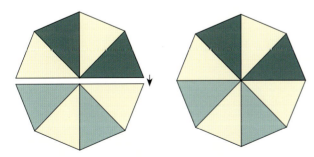

Make 3 Partial Butterfly Wings Units.

5 Cut one Partial Butterfly Wings Unit in half and gently trim ⅛" from the center on each side to make room for the Butterfly Body Unit.

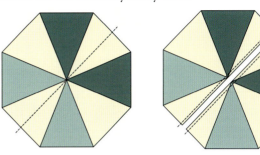

Make 6 Butterfly Wings Units.

6 Assemble two matching Butterfly Wings Units and one Butterfly Body Unit.

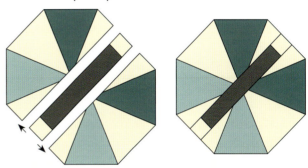

Make 3 Butterfly Units.

7 Assemble four Fabric B triangles and one Butterfly Unit.

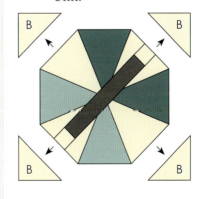 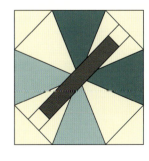

Make 3 Butterfly Blocks.
8 ½" x 8 ½" unfinished.

8 To add the antennae, use three strands of embroidery floss and a stem stitch.

Template is on page 113.

Make 1. 8 ½" x 60 ½" unfinished.

42260-12   42262-24   42260-22   42261-32

Edyta's Tips:

Strip piecing can save you time when making multiples of the same unit. To make the fence crossbars in this block, strip piece first and then subcut your pieces.

Fabric Requirements:

Background ½ yard	Fabrics A to D
Fence ⅝ yard	Fabrics E to J
Crossbars ¼ yard	Fabric K
Fence Accent One 10" square	Fabric L

Cutting:

Background

3 - 3" x width of fabric strips, subcut into:
  2 - 3" x width of fabric strips (A)
  2 - 2" x 3" rectangles (B)

3 - 1 ½" x width of fabric strips, subcut into:
  1 - 1 ½" x width of fabric strip (C)
  38 - 1 ½" squares (D)

Fence

1 - 3 ½" x width of fabric strip, subcut into:
  1 - 3 ½" x 4" rectangle (E)

4 - 2 ½" x width of fabric strips, subcut into:
  16 - 2 ½" x 8 ½" rectangles (F)
  1 - 2 ½" x 3 ½" rectangle (G)

1 - 2" x width of fabric strip, subcut into:
  2 - 2" x 8 ½" rectangles (H)
  2 - 2" squares (I)
  4 - 1" squares (J)

Crossbars

  2 - 1 ½" x width of fabric strips (K)

Fence Accent

  2 - 2 ½" x 8 ½" rectangles (L)

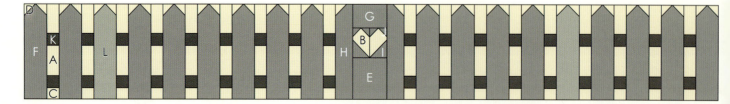

Construction:

1 Assemble two Fabric A strips, two Fabric K strips and the Fabric C strip.

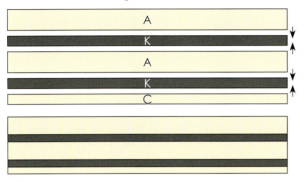

Make 1 Fence Strip Set.
8 ½" x 42" unfinished.

2 Subcut the Fence Strip Set into eighteen 1 ½" x 8 ½" rectangles.

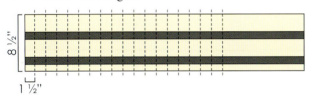

Make 18 Crossbar Units.
1 ½" x 8 ½" unfinished.

3 Draw a diagonal line on the wrong side of the Fabric D squares.

With right sides facing, layer a Fabric D square on the top left corner of a Fabric F rectangle.

Stitch on the drawn line and trim ¼" away from the seam.

Repeat on the top right corner.

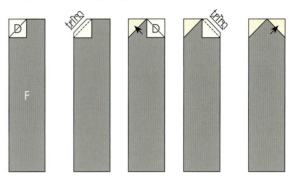

Make 16 Large Fence Post Units.
2 ½" x 8 ½" unfinished.

4 With right sides facing, layer a Fabric D square on the top left corner of a Fabric L rectangle.

Stitch on the drawn line and trim ¼" away from the seam.

Repeat on the top right corner.

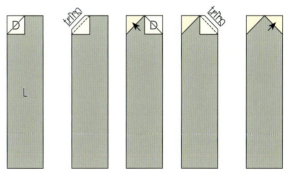

Make 2 Alternate Large Fence Post Units.
2 ½" x 8 ½" unfinished.

5 With right sides facing, layer a Fabric D square on the top left corner of a Fabric H rectangle.

Stitch on the drawn line and trim ¼" away from the seam.

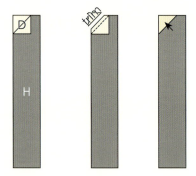

Make 1 Left Small Fence Post Unit.
2" x 8 ½" unfinished.

6 With right sides facing, layer a Fabric D square on the top right corner of a Fabric H rectangle.

Stitch on the drawn line and trim ¼" away from the seam.

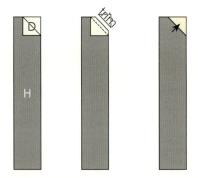

Make 1 Right Small Fence Post Unit.
2" x 8 ½" unfinished.

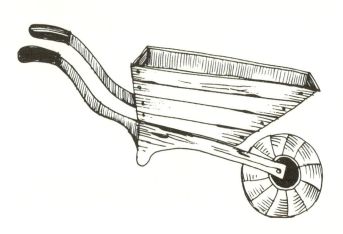

7 Draw a diagonal line on the wrong side of the Fabric J squares and the Fabric I squares.

With right sides facing, layer a Fabric J square on the top left corner of a Fabric B rectangle.

Stitch on the drawn line and trim ¼" away from the seam.

Repeat on the top right corner with a Fabric J square and the bottom end with a Fabric I square.

Make 1 Left Heart Unit.
2" x 3" unfinished.

8 With right sides facing, layer a Fabric J square on the top left corner of a Fabric B rectangle.

Stitch on the drawn line and trim ¼" away from the seam.

Repeat on the top right corner with a Fabric J square and the bottom end with a Fabric I square.

Make 1 Right Heart Unit.
2" x 3" unfinished.

9 Assemble the Fabric G rectangle, the Left Heart Unit, the Right Heart Unit and the Fabric E rectangle.

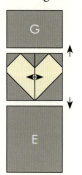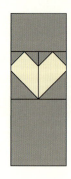

Make 1 Center Fence Post Unit.
3 ½" x 8 ½" unfinished.

10 Assemble sixteen Large Fence Post Units, eighteen Crossbar Units, two Alternate Large Fence Post Units, the Left Small Fence Post Unit, the Center Fence Post Unit and the Right Small Fence Post Unit. Press toward the Crossbar Units.

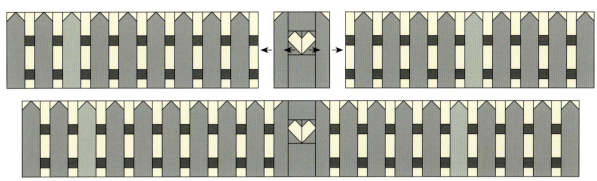

Make 1 Fence Block.
8 ½" x 60 ½" unfinished.

Fabric Requirements:

75" x 78 ½"

Background 2 ½ yards	Fabrics A to Y
Flower Pot Fabric One 10" square	Fabric Z
Rake Handle & Flower Pot Fabric ⅜ yard	Fabrics Z & AA

Top Rake & Flower Pot Fabric Fat Eighth (9" x 21")	Fabrics Z, BB & CC
Top Rake & Watering Can Fabric Fat Eighth (9" x 21")	Fabrics DD to JJ
Watering Can Base Fabric One 10" square	Fabric KK

42260-12   42262-24   42267-21   42260-22   42261-32   42265-34

Cutting:

Background

2 - 8 ½" x width of fabric strips, subcut into:
- 1 - 8 ½" x 42" strip (A)
- 1 - 8 ½" x 32 ½" strip (B)

2 - 8" x width of fabric strips, sew end to end and subcut into:
- 1 - 8" x 67 ½" strip (C)

1 - 7 ½" x width of fabric strip, subcut into:
- 1 - 7 ½" x 20" rectangle (D)

2 - 6 ½" x width of fabric strips, sew end to end and subcut into:
- 1 - 6 ½" x 50" strip (E)

1 - 5 ½" x width of fabric strip, subcut into:
- 1 - 5 ½" x 10" rectangle (F)
- 1 - 5 ½" x 10" rectangle (G)

2 - 5" x width of fabric strips, sew end to end and subcut into:
- 1 - 5" x 50 ½" strip (H)
- 1 - 4 ½" x 8 ½" rectangle (I)

1 - 3 ½" x width of fabric strip, subcut into:
- 1 - 3 ½" x 14 ½" rectangle (J)
- 1 - 3 ½" x 5" rectangle (K)
- 1 - 3 ½" x 4" rectangle (L)
- 1 - 3" x 11" rectangle (M)
- 1 - 3" x 3 ½" rectangle (N)

3 - 2" x width of fabric strips, sew end to end and subcut into:
- 1 - 2" x 50 ½" strip (O)
- 1 - 2" x 4" rectangle (P)
- 2 - 2" x 3 ½" rectangles (Q)
- 9 - 2" x 2 ½" rectangles (R)
- 5 - 2" squares (S)

1 - 1 ½" x width of fabric strip, subcut into:
- 1 - 1 ½" x 11" rectangle (T)
- 1 - 1 ½" x 7 ½" rectangle (U)
- 1 - 1 ½" x 5" rectangle (V)
- 1 - 1 ½" x 3" rectangle (W)
- 1 - 1 ½" x 2" rectangle (X)
- 3 - 1 ½" squares (Y)

Flower Pot Fabric
- 1 - 5 ½" x 6" rectangle (Z)

Rake Handle & Flower Pot Fabric

1 - 5 ½" x width of fabric strip, subcut into:
- 1 - 5 ½" x 6" rectangle (Z)

2 - 1 ½" x width of fabric strips, sew end to end and subcut into:
- 1 - 1 ½" x 50 ½" strip (AA)

Top Rake & Flower Pot Fabric
- 1 - 5 ½" x 6" rectangle (Z)
- 1 - 1" x 11" rectangle (BB)
- 1 - 1" x 6 ½" rectangle (CC)

Top Rake & Watering Can Fabric
- 1 - 3 ½" square (DD)
- 1 - 2" x 3 ½" rectangle (EE)
- 3 - 2" squares (FF)
- 1 - 1" x 5" rectangle (GG)
- 1 - 1" x 3 ½" rectangle (HH)
- 9 - 1" x 2 ½" rectangles (II)
- 1 - 1" x 2" rectangle (JJ)

Watering Can Base Fabric
- 1 - 6 ½" x 8 ½" rectangle (KK)

Flower Pot Templates
- Templates are on page 114.

Construction:

Quilt Rows:

1   Assemble three Butterfly Blocks, the Fabric I rectangle and the Fabric B strip.

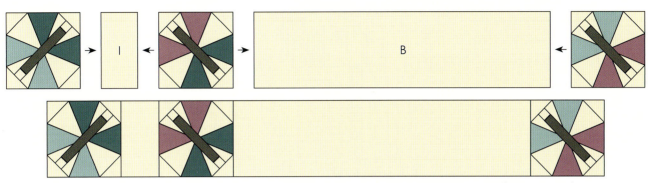

Make 1 First Quilt Row.
8 ½" x 60 ½" unfinished.

2   Assemble the Bachelor Button Block, the Sweet Pea Block, the Moon Flower Block, the Petunias Block and the Honeysuckle Block.

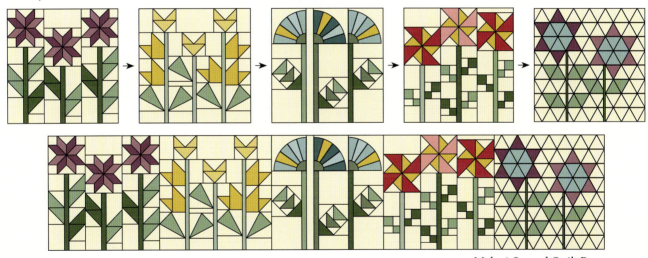

Make 1 Second Quilt Row.
12 ½" x 60 ½" unfinished.

3 Assemble the Nine Patch Daisy Block, the Dahlia Block, the Daylily Block, the Coneflower Block, the Hollyhock Block, the Greenhouse Block and the Sunflower Block.

Make 1 Third Quilt Row.
24 ½" x 60 ½" unfinished.

4 Assemble the Cosmos Block, the Tulips Block, the Sidewalk and Log Cabin Roses Block, the Delphiniums Block and the Cat Block.

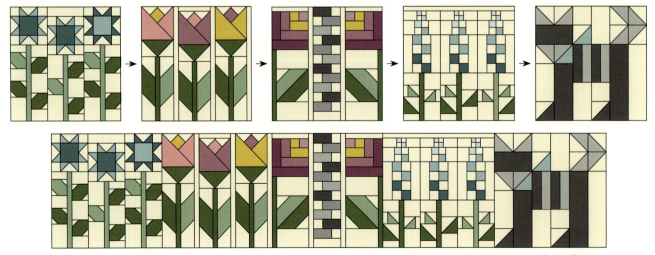

Make 1 Fourth Quilt Row.
12 ½" x 60 ½" unfinished.

Quilt Center:

1 Assemble the Quilt Center.

Make 1 Quilt Center.
60 ½" x 64 ½" unfinished.

Top Border:

1   Assemble six Fabric II rectangles, five Fabric R rectangles, the Fabric T rectangle, the Fabric BB rectangle and the Fabric M rectangle.

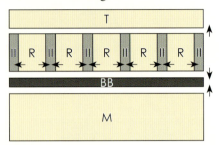

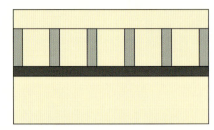

Make 1 Top Right Rake Unit.
6 ½" x 11" unfinished.

2   Assemble the Top Right Rake Unit and the Fabric E strip.

Make 1 Top Border.
6 ½" x 60 ½" unfinished.

Bottom Border:

1   Using the Left Flower Pot Template, cut three Left Flower Pot Units.

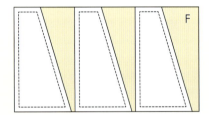

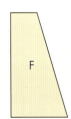

Make 3 Left Flower Pot Units.

2   Using the Right Flower Pot Template, cut three Right Flower Pot Units.

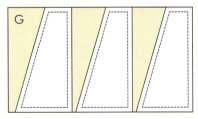

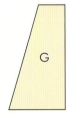

Make 3 Right Flower Pot Units.

3 Using the Center Flower Pot Template, cut three different Center Flower Pot Units.

Make 3 Center Flower Pot Units.

4 Assemble one Left Flower Pot Unit, one Center Flower Pot Unit and one Right Flower Pot Unit.

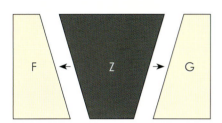 

Make 3 Flower Pot Units.
5 ½" x 7 ½" unfinished.

5 Assemble two Flower Pot Units and the Fabric J rectangle.

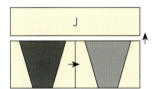 

Make 1 Left Bottom Border Unit.
8 ½" x 14 ½" unfinished.

6 Draw a diagonal line on the wrong side of the Fabric DD square.

With right sides facing, layer the Fabric DD square on the bottom end of the Fabric K rectangle.

Stitch on the drawn line and trim ¼" away from the seam.

Make 1 Top Left Spout Unit.
3 ½" x 5" unfinished.

7 Draw a diagonal line on the wrong side of the Fabric S squares.

With right sides facing, layer a Fabric S square on the top end of the Fabric EE rectangle.

Stitch on the drawn line and trim ¼" away from the seam.

Repeat on the bottom end.

Make 1 Middle Right Spout Unit.
2" x 3 ½" unfinished.

8 Assemble the Top Left Spout Unit, the Fabric L rectangle, one Fabric Q rectangle, the Middle Right Spout Unit and one Fabric R rectangle.

Make 1 Spout Unit.
5" x 8 ½" unfinished.

9 Assemble the Left Bottom Border Unit, the Fabric A strip and the Spout Unit.

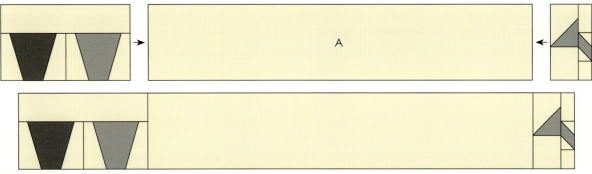

Make 1 Bottom Border.
8 ½" x 60 ½" unfinished.

Left Border:

1 Assemble three Fabric II rectangles, three Fabric R rectangles and the Fabric CC rectangle.

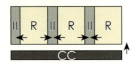 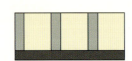

Make 1 Top Left Rake Unit.
3" x 6 ½" unfinished.

2 Assemble the Fabric W rectangle, the Top Left Rake Unit and the Fabric U rectangle.

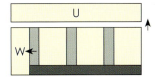
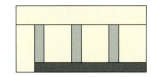

Make 1 Top Left Border Unit.
4" x 7 ½" unfinished.

3 Assemble the Fabric H strip, the Fabric AA strip, the Fabric O strip, the Top Left Border Unit, the Fabric D rectangle and one Flower Pot Unit.

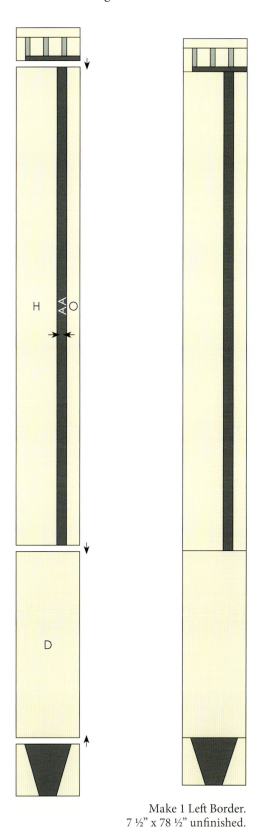

Make 1 Left Border.
7 ½" x 78 ½" unfinished.

Right Border:

1. Draw a diagonal line on the wrong side of the Fabric Y squares.

   With right sides facing, layer a Fabric S square with a Fabric FF square.

   Stitch on the drawn line and trim ¼" away from the seam.

   Repeat on the bottom right corner with a Fabric Y square.

   Make 3 Side Handle Units.
   2" x 2" unfinished.

2. Assemble the Fabric JJ rectangle, the Fabric X rectangle and one Side Handle Unit.

   Make 1 Partial Top Handle Unit.
   2" x 3 ½" unfinished.

3. Assemble the Fabric HH rectangle, the Fabric N rectangle, one Fabric Q rectangle and the Partial Top Handle Unit.

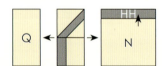 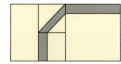

   Make 1 Top Handle Unit.
   3 ½" x 6 ½" unfinished.

4. Assemble the Fabric V rectangle, the Fabric GG rectangle, two Side Handle Units and the Fabric P rectangle.

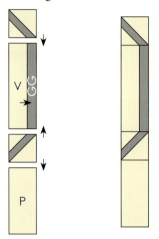

   Make 1 Right Handle Unit.
   2" x 11 ½" unfinished.

5. Assemble the Top Handle Unit, the Fabric KK rectangle and the Right Handle Unit.

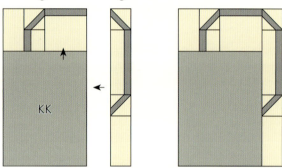

   Make 1 Bottom Right Border Unit.
   8" x 11 ½" unfinished.

6 Assemble the Fabric C strip and the Bottom Right Border Unit.

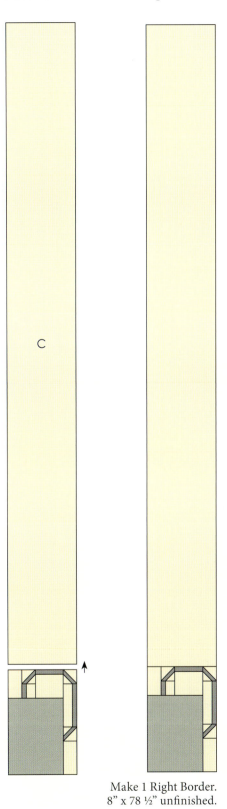

Make 1 Right Border.
8" x 78 ½" unfinished.

Borders:

1   Attach the Top Border and the Bottom Border. Attach the Left Border and the Right Border.

75" x 78 ½"

Fabric Requirements:

Flower Petals
Four 10" squares   Fabric A

Bird Wing   Fabrics G & H
One 10" square

Flower Centers   Fabric B
One 10" square

Black Embroidery Floss

Vines, Stems and Leaves   Fabrics C & D
Three Fat Quarters (18" x 21")

⅜" Bias Tape Maker

Bird Body   Fabrics E & F
One 10" square

42268-46 42265-40 42261-42 42264-34 42265-44 42262-38 42261-38 42266-30 42261-36 42266-20

Cutting:

Flower Petals
16 - Flower Petals total (A)

Flower Centers
16 - Flower Centers (B)

Vines, Stems and Leaves - from one fabric cut
12 - Leaves (C)
1 - ¾" x 14" Bias Strip (D)

Vines, Stems and Leaves - from one fabric cut
12 - Leaves (C)
5 - ¾" x 14" Bias Strips (D)

Vines, Stems and Leaves - from one fabric cut
11 - Leaves (C)
6 - ¾" x 14" Bias Strips (D)

Bird Body
2 - Left Bird Bodies (E)
2 - Right Bird Bodies (F)

Bird Wing
2 - Left Bird Wings (G)
2 - Right Bird Wings (H)

Applique Templates
Templates are on page 102.

Applique:

1   Sew the Fabric D bias strips end to end for the vines and stems. Using a ⅜" bias tape maker, prepare the Fabric D bias strips. Using the Vines and Stems template, subcut your vines and flower stems to desired length.

2   Cut the Flower Petals, Flower Centers, Leaves, Bird Bodies and Bird Wings. Using your applique method of choice, prepare the applique pieces.

3   Position the applique pieces on the quilt top according the placement guide below. Using your applique method of choice, applique in place.

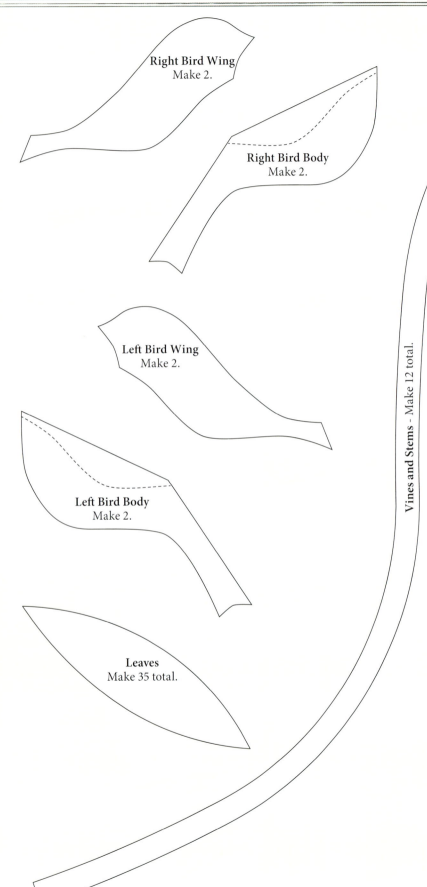

Right Bird Wing
Make 2.

Right Bird Body
Make 2.

Left Bird Wing
Make 2.

Left Bird Body
Make 2.

Leaves
Make 35 total.

Vines and Stems - Make 12 total.

Flower Centers
Make 16.

Flower Petals
Make 16 total.

Embroidery:

1 To add the words "Quilters Patch" and the year, use the templates on pages 104 to 106.

2 Following the placement diagram below, use three strands of embroidery floss and a stem stitch. Instructions for the stem stitch are on page 5.

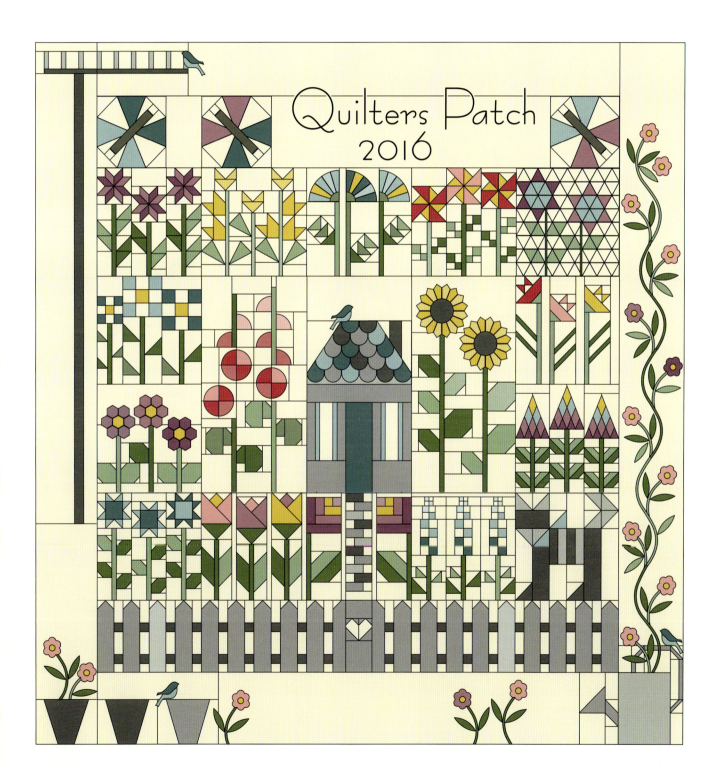

Qui
Q
P

lters

atch

0 1 2 3

4 5 6

7 8 9

BINDING & BACKING

Fabric Requirements:

Binding
⅞ yard

Fabric A

Backing
7 ⅜ yards

Fabric B

42261-36   42267-12

Cutting:

Binding
9 - 2 ½" x width of fabric strips (A)

Backing
3 - 29" x 88 ½" strips (B)

Quilting:

1   Sew three Fabric B strips together using a ½" seam allowance.

2   Layer quilt in the following order:

1. Quilt Back (right side down) - 85" x 88 ½"

2. Batting (I prefer Hobbs for best results) - 85" x 88 ½"

3. Quilt Top (right side up) - 75" x 78 ½"

3   Baste layers together.

4   Quilt by hand or machine.

Binding:

1   Trim the batting and backing even with the Quilt Top.

2   Piece the Fabric A strips together end to end or on the diagonal to create one long strip.

3   After folding the strip in half wrong sides together, place the binding strip on top of the quilt so the raw edges align on the outside edge of the quilt.

4   Sew along the edge of the entire quilt to attach the binding to the quilt.

5   When sewing, stop ¼" away from corner, reposition the binding to align with the next quilt side, and continue sewing.

6   Fold the binding around the outer edge of the quilt and sew it to the back of the quilt.

Dahlia Block
Page 36
¾" Hexagon
Template

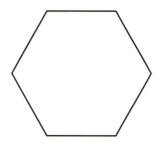

Dahlia Block - Page 36
¾" Paper Template

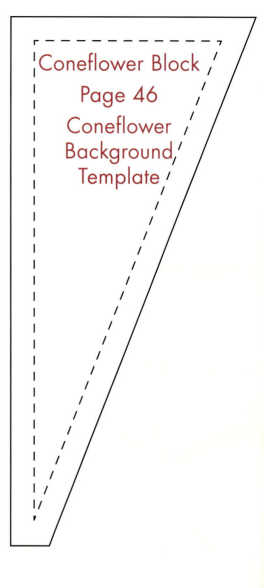

Coneflower Block
Page 46
Coneflower
Background
Template

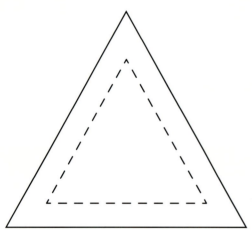

Honeysuckle Block - Page 42
60° Triangle Template

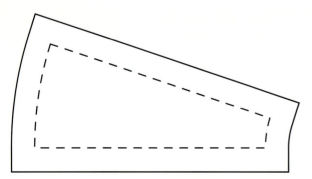

Moon Flower Block - Page 52
Moon Flower Template

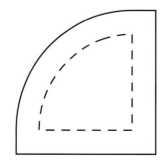

Moon Flower Block
Page 52
Moon Flower Stem
Template

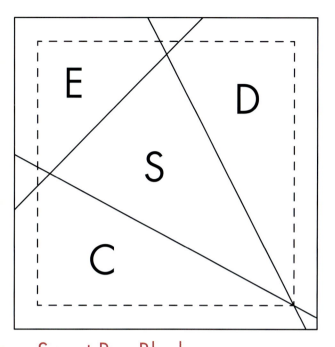

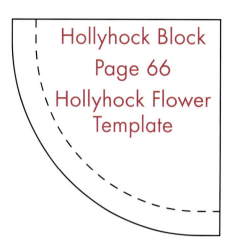

Hollyhock Block
Page 66
Hollyhock Flower
Template

Sweet Pea Block
Page 58
Sweet Pea Leaf Paper
Piecing Template

E

D

S

C

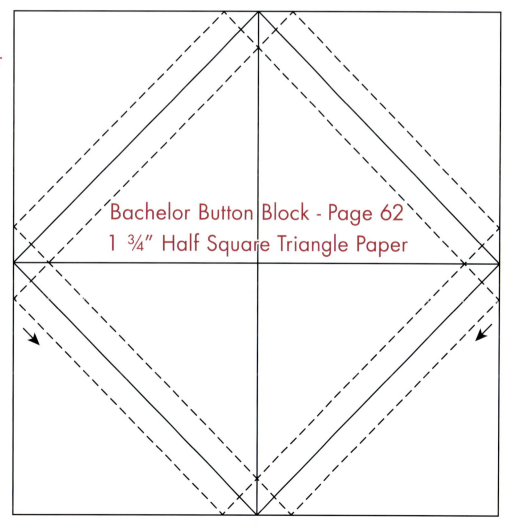

Bachelor Button Block - Page 62
1 ¾" Half Square Triangle Paper

Greenhouse Block - Page 72
Right Background Roof Template

Greenhouse Block - Page 72
Left Background Roof Template

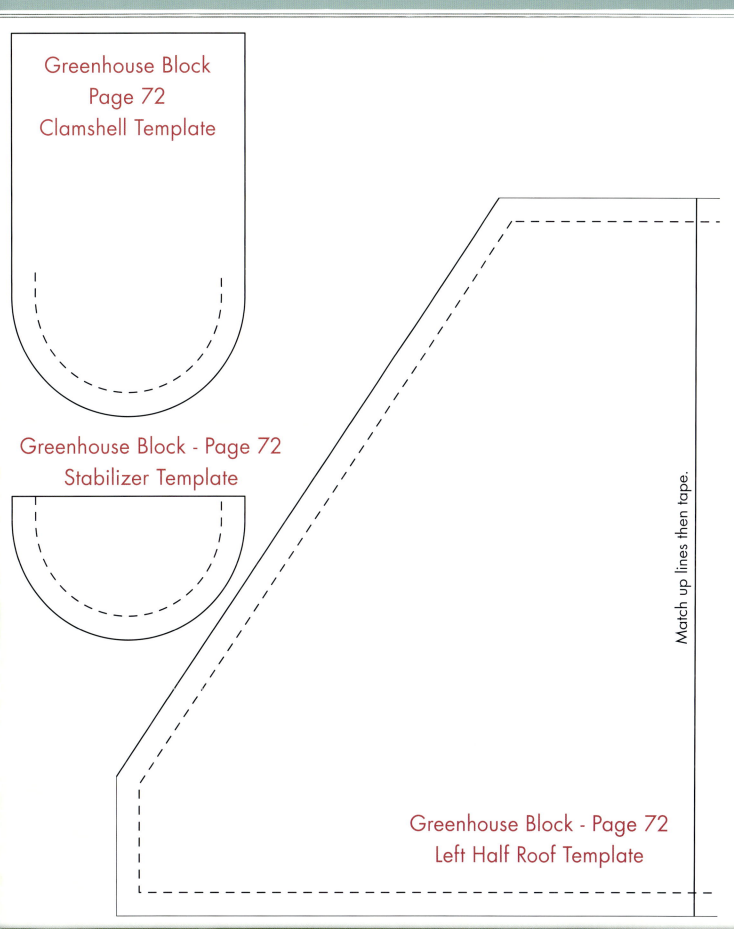

Greenhouse Block
Page 72
Clamshell Template

Greenhouse Block - Page 72
Stabilizer Template

Match up lines then tape.

Greenhouse Block - Page 72
Left Half Roof Template

Match up lines then tape.

Greenhouse Block - Page 72
Right Half Roof Template

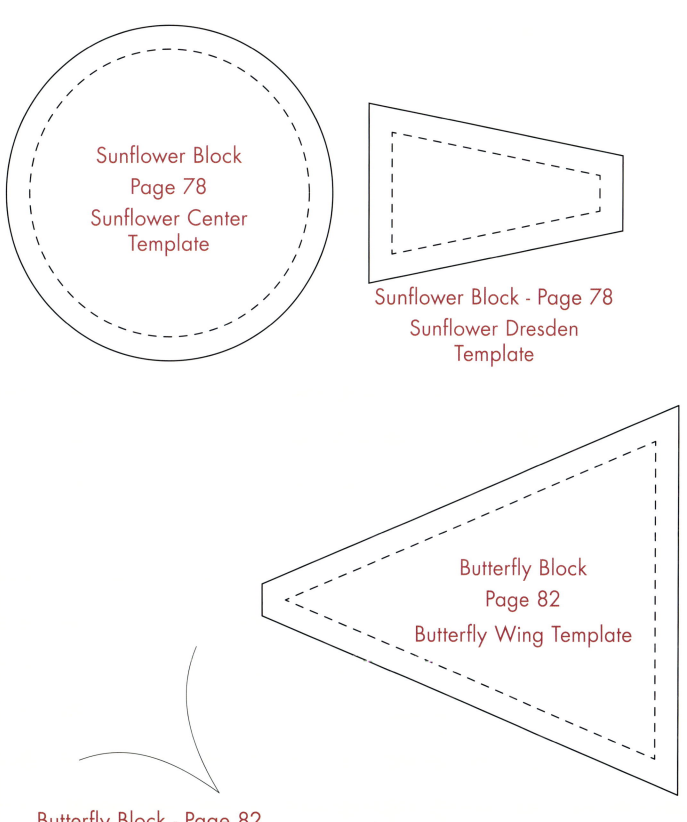

Sunflower Block
Page 78
Sunflower Center
Template

Sunflower Block - Page 78
Sunflower Dresden
Template

Butterfly Block
Page 82
Butterfly Wing Template

Butterfly Block - Page 82
Antennae Embroidery Template

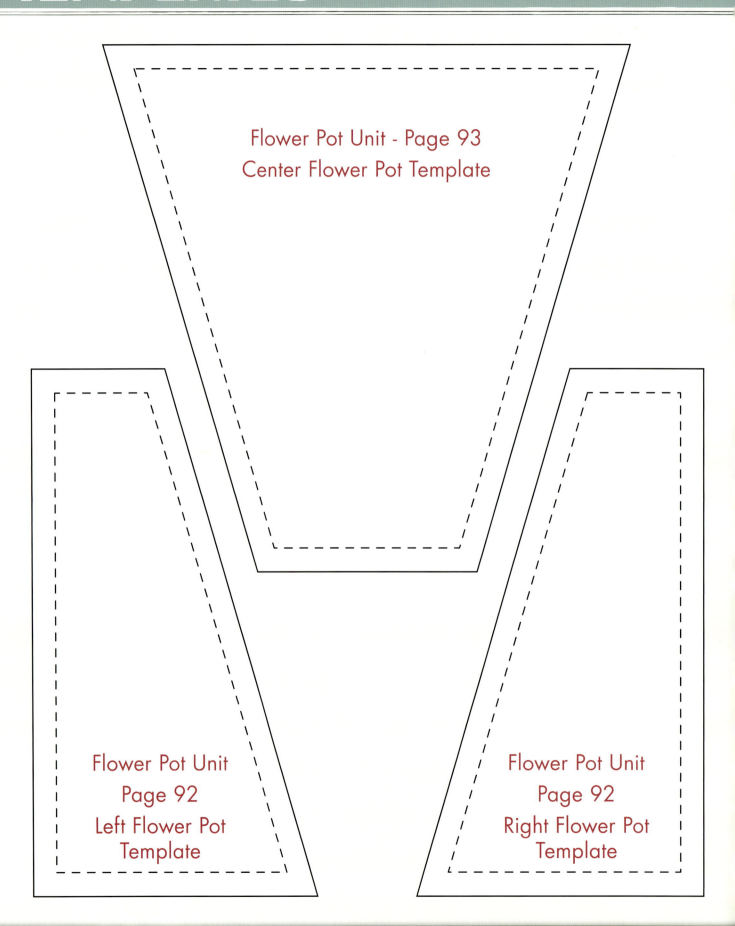

Flower Pot Unit - Page 93
Center Flower Pot Template

Flower Pot Unit
Page 92
Left Flower Pot
Template

Flower Pot Unit
Page 92
Right Flower Pot
Template

Silver Linings in Color

Fabric collection by Edyta Sitar of Laundry Basket Quilts for Moda Fabrics

42260-12
5 ½ yards

42266-12
1 yard

42265-34
⅓ yard

42261-32
1 yard

42266-20
⅓ yard

42268-12
2 ⅞ yards

42267-12
1 yard
Backing: 7 ⅜ yards

42262-24
1 ⅛ yards

42260-22
1 yard

42267-21
⅜ yard

42268-44
⅔ yard

42264-39
⅓ yard

42261-37
⅓ yard

42260-31
¾ yard

42261-36
⅓ yard
Binding: ⅞ yard

42266-30
1 ¾ yards

42262-38
1 ¼ yards

42265-27
¾ yard

42261-38
2 ½ yards

42265-44
¾ yard

42268-50
1 yard

42268-46
⅓ yard

42264-41
⅔ yard

42265-40
⅓ yard

42261-42
1 yard

42264-34
¾ yard

42267-32
10" x WOF